THE HEALTH AND SAFETY HANDBOOK

by

GARETH WATKINS

LONDON
SWEET & MAXWELL
1997

Published in 1997 by
Sweet & Maxwell Ltd of
100 Avenue Road,
London NW3 3PF
Typeset by York House Typographic Ltd, London W13 8NT
Printed in Great Britain by Headway Press Ltd, Reading

No natural forests were destroyed to make this product;
only farmed timber was used and replanted

A CIP catalogue record for this book is available from the
British Library

ISBN 0 421 583 304

DEDICATION

For Janice.

PREFACE

The idea for this book arose at a health and safety seminar, at which I had been speaking. During one of the breaks, I was chatting to a friend and bemoaning the limited time available for speakers to get their ideas across. So much to say, and so little time to say it. "You should write a book", said my friend. So I did.

Although written by a lawyer, this is not a book just for other lawyers (at least not unless they also happen to be responsible for health and safety). Neither is it a textbook. It is a practical book for practical people. It is intended to be of use to anyone who needs to have regard to the application of legal requirements to health and safety in the workplace, and particularly to managers who carry legal responsibilities. In writing this book I have sought to draw, not only upon the strict requirements of the law, but also upon nearly 20 years' experience of advising and representing managers and employers in connection with every conceivable legal forum or investigation arising out of health and safety law. In addition, of course, I have also drawn heavily upon the thoughts and teachings of others. Those whose ideas have most closely influenced my own thinking include Frank Widdowson, formerly legal adviser to the British Coal Corporation on health, safety and the environment; my partners Tom Symes and Carl Dray; Bob Wright, chairman of the British Standards Society; and consultants Bob Mitchell and Bruce Staley. I am particularly indebted to Professor Richard Booth of Aston University for his work on risk assessment. These, along with many others, have shaped my thinking on the subject matter of this book. Whether they have shaped it in the right direction is a matter for others to judge, but I am grateful to them. They cannot, of course, be held responsible for any errors or faults in this book—I claim sole credit for those.

Finally, my warmest thanks to Lyn McPherson for her research and support, particularly in relation to Chapter 16; to my secretary

Helen Rutledge for typing the manuscript and being an all round godsend; and to my wife Janice for—well, for being my wife Janice.

Gareth Watkins
Sheffield

May 1997

CONTENTS

TABLE OF CASES

(References are to paragraph numbers)

TABLE OF STATUTES

*(References are to paragraph numbers; references in **bold** type denote material set out in the Appendices)*

xv

TABLE OF STATUTORY INSTRUMENTS

*(References are to paragraph numbers; references in **bold** denote material set out in the Appendices)*

TABLE OF EUROPEAN LEGISLATION

CHAPTER 1

HEALTH AND SAFETY 2000

Introduction

The twentieth century has been a period of extraordinary change in   **1–01**
working practices and conditions, as it has in almost every other
aspect of life. Changes in the legal environment regulating safety
have been just as dramatic.

At the start of this century no workman in the United Kingdom
could recover compensation for an injury at work if he had, by his
own neglect, made any contribution to the accident. Neither could he
recover from his employer if the accident was due to the neglect of a
fellow employee. As we move into the twenty-first century the
position could not be more different, with companies being convicted
of manslaughter and directors having been imprisoned and disqualified for safety-related offences.

Although there have been great advances in safety standards,
particularly during the second half of the century, new working
practices and technology have brought with them new dangers —
and new industrial diseases. The legal environment for employers
during the twenty-first century looks set fair to be a tough one. The
courts, building upon legislative changes over the last decade, have
demonstrated a determination to give health and safety requirements their widest possible interpretation and effect.

The Labour Market

1–02 The dominating feature of commerce and industry in the 1990s has been the change in traditional patterns of employment. There has been a sharp movement away from the employer — employee relationship upon which, historically, most health and safety law and practice has been based. In its place have arisen a variety of relationships and strategies — contractorisation, outsourcing, facilities management and "de-layering". In tandem with these developments there has been an increase in leisure facilities and the attention paid to management of public sector services where safety is a key issue — hospitals, schools, and leisure centres, for example. What all these movements have in common is that they bring about situations where those with the duty to ensure safety are often not the employers of those whose safety is to be ensured. Whilst this is not a new situation, the scale and frequency with which it arises certainly is.

The Agents of Change

1–03 In considering the factors behind the shifting legal environment, two areas stand out. The first of these is the unusually high level of major civil disasters which occurred in the United Kingdom during the latter half of the 1980s. These disasters, some of them now indelibly etched on the national psyche, include the capsizal of the Herald of Free Enterprise, Piper Alpha, Hillsborough, Clapham Junction, the Manchester plane fire, the sinking of the Marchioness and the Kings Cross fire. The combined effect of these events has been to drive health and safety, as an issue, first up the media agenda and then up the political agenda. Eventually the concerns generated by events such as these have reached the judicial agenda. It should also be noted that a number of the judges who dealt with the public inquiries into these incidents are now in senior positions in the Court of Appeal and are able to reflect, in their decisions, the lessons which they assimilated during those inquiries.

The second factor in the changing legal environment is the replacement of unanimous voting on health and safety directives in the European Union by a system of majority voting amongst member states. This change, ushered in by the Single European Act in 1987, has removed a veto on health and safety directives from the hands of individual states and freed up the mechanisms within the European Union to produce further directives — which in turn have to be implemented by the United Kingdom's own Parliament. The effect of this change can very easily be seen when one considers that between 1970 and 1985 only six health and safety directives were adopted by the European Union, whereas since the Single European Act well over 20 directives with some relevance to health and safety have been adopted. In particular, amongst these directives were the measures which led to the implementation of the "six-pack" regulations in the United Kingdom in 1993 (see Appendices 7 to 12). For good or ill it is the European Union which is in the driving seat so far as new legislation is concerned, and its executive arm, the European Commission, has been driving matters forward at a cracking pace.

The Pace of Change

The pace of change has picked up considerably in recent years with a **1–04** number of important precedents being set. Probably one of the most significant decisions in health and safety law this century was that in *R. v. Oll* (*Health and Safety Bulletin* 229, January 1995) which resulted in the first ever conviction for manslaughter of a company in the United Kingdom. That case arose out of the drowning of four teenagers off Lyme Bay in a canoeing accident in 1993. During this century there had been three previous attempts to convict corporate bodies of the crime of manslaughter (the most recent following the capsizal of the Herald of Free Enterprise), but all had ended in acquittals. In a case arising from the same set of facts, *R. v. Kyte* (*Health and Safety Bulletin* 229, January 1995), the managing director of the defendant company was convicted of manslaughter personally and sentenced to three years imprisonment, later reduced to two years on appeal. That sentence represented the first occasion on which a company director had been sentenced to an immediate term of imprisonment following a manslaughter conviction. It was, in fact, only the second such conviction ever, the first occurring as recently as 1989.

In *R. v. Hill* (*Health and Safety Bulletin* 243, March 1996) the defendant, who was a demolition contractor, was sentenced to three months imprisonment for failing to take adequate precautions to minimise asbestos contamination during the demolition process. Once again the case sets an important precedent as it is the first occasion on which a defendant has been given an immediate prison term for a breach of the regulations made under the Health and Safety at Work Act. In another demolition case, *R. v. Glen* (*Legal Times*, November 16, 1994), the defendant became the first independent health and safety consultant to be convicted of an offence under section 3 of the Health and Safety at Work Act (see Appendix 6), in that he failed to ensure that work was carried out in accordance with a method statement which he had drafted. In addition to these cases we have also witnessed record fines under the Health and Safety at Work Act against both companies and individuals.

1–05   As the use of outsourcing and contractorisation has increased, so the focus of ground-breaking prosecutions has shifted from section 2 of the Health and Safety at Work Act (responsibility to an organisation's own employees) to section 3 (liability towards those not employed by the organisation but affected by it) — see Appendix 6. One important example of this trend in cases is *R. v. Associated Octel* ([1994] 4 All E.R. 1051, C.A.) (see Chapter 8), decided in 1994. In that case the defendants were found guilty under section 3 in respect of an accident to an employee of a contactor. This was despite the fact that the defendant relied upon the skill and expertise of the contractor, who had control of the way in which the work was carried out. Another important example occurred in the case of *R. v. British Steel* ([1995] 1 W.L.R. 1356) where the defendant was found guilty under section 3 in relation to a fatal accident sustained by a contractor's employee. This was on the grounds that the defendant was liable for the negligent supervision of the contractors by one of its own managers and that, even had the defendant taken all necessary precautions at the level of senior management or the "controlling mind" of the company, this would not amount to a defence on a charge under section 3 of the Health and Safety at Work Act.

1–06   These cases represent a changing attitude towards health and safety by the judiciary and, taken as a whole, demonstrate a determination to make a proactive contribution towards improving health and safety standards. The cases demonstrate that judges perceive themselves as having an important role to play in improving standards and that they are prepared to impose severe sentences in appropriate cases and also to give the wording of legislation its widest possible meaning. The ability of employers to demonstrate compliance with legal standards, and the necessity to keep those standards under constant review, are more important than ever.

CHAPTER 2

COUNTING THE COST

The Financial Cost of Injury and Ill-Health

The cost of industrial accidents and occupational diseases is most **2–01** easily measured in human misery and tears. We can all understand that because we are all — we and our families — potential victims of accidents and disasters. The senior manager, however, must also look objectively at the financial cost of injury and ill-health. Safety in the workplace is, among other things, a bottom line issue. We operate our businesses in increasingly competitive times. As our costs increase we find that there is an element which we cannot pass on to our customers — thereby putting pressure on our margins. Savings in the costs of safety — or rather the costs of lack of safety — can make a material difference to profitability. At the margins, and after other costs have been accounted for, every pound saved is an extra pound of trading profit.

The potential difficulty lies in accurately estimating the true cost to the business of accidents and ill health, and therefore calculating and then measuring any savings. Many estimates have been made in relation to specific incidents, usually by relatively large companies who have in-house resources to undertake what can be a very complex exercise. BP have estimated the total cost of a refinery fire at Grangemouth in 1987 at about £100 million, including business interruption costs. The cost of the Piper Alpha explosion and fire is recokoned at about £2 billion. However, the great majority of the aggregate cost to industry of ill health consists not of a few well-publicised incidents, but of the cumulative effect of a high number of more routine incidents. Often the costs are obscured by increases in

5

maintenance costs and insurance premiums; the extra salary costs of covering injury-induced absences; and the extra administative costs of investigations, dealing with personnel issues and satisfying the insatiable demands of lawyers.

2–02 In "The Costs of Accidents at Work" (HS (G) 96) the HSE published the results of five case studies undertaken by its Accident Prevention Advisory Unit in 1990 and 1991. The case studies, carried out with the co-operation of the employers concerned, sought to measure the true economic cost to employers of a number of specific incidents. The employers also agreed on the methodology. The case studies covered a range of employers and featured a construction site, the food sector, transport, energy and the public sector.

The results of the studies are very instructive, with the cost of accidents being calculated, variously as 37 per cent of profits; 1.4 per cent of operating costs; 8.55 per cent of tender price; 5 per cent of annual running costs; and 14.2 per cent of potential output. The uninsured costs of accidents varied between eight times and 36 times the insured costs (*i.e.* the insurance premiums).

These figures suggest that material savings in the costs of accidents could bring substantial financial benefits. Of course, the scope for savings is limited. In the long run no organisation can expect to cut its accident costs to zero, because some level of accidents is a statistical inevitability. But, somewhere between the existing level of cost and zero cost there is a realistic area of potential saving that no senior manager can afford to ignore.

Categorising Your Risks and Performance

2–03 A manager's view of what strategy to adopt in seeking to make savings in the costs of accidents will depend, in part at least, on his perception of the inherent levels of risk generated by the business and the business's performance in controlling those risks. In thinking about where you are now, and where you might want to get to, it may be useful to categorise your business. Firstly into high risk or low risk and secondly into good or poor safety performance relative to those risks. These categories can be represented on a simple risk/performance model, shown in Table 1.

Employers will aim to move towards the left-hand boxes of Table 1, improving performance and generating savings, either the top or

Table 1

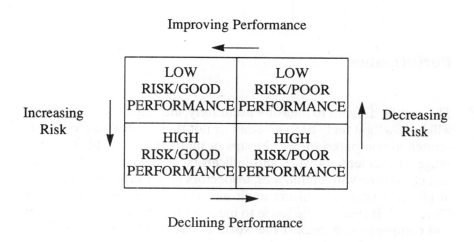

bottom box depending upon the nature of the business. Of course, it's a rough-and-ready approach but a useful starting point in stimulating the thinking process for those working or re-working their safety and their business strategies.

Risk

Categorising businesses as high or low level risk will be a reasonably **2–04** straightforward task for most employers, but not for all as some organisations will fall close to the borderline or, if diverse, will fall into both boxes. In this latter case the different elements of the business should be separated out and considered individually.

Into the high risk box will fall business where the likelihood of accidents or ill-health is relatively high or where the consequences if accidents do occur will be severe, leading to serious injury or death. Working with hazardous substances such as nuclear materials or chemicals deserves a high risk status. So does working in a hostile environment — underground, underwater or in the air — as does working in close proximity to powerful machinery or equipment.

Employers in the commercial, retail or leisure sectors will generally be in the low risk box, although it would be unwise to generalise. Some leisure activities generate quite high levels of risk, particularly those engaged in outdoor activities or featuring water.

Performance

2–05 This can be difficult to measure accurately, although most employers will have a "gut feel" as to whether or not their performance is up to scratch as compared to peer groups or industry norms. Measuring a range of accident statistics and indicators, benchmarking exercises, and consulting with employees, inspectors and insurers will all assist in taking a view, as will the audit and review exercises outlined in Chapter 7. It makes little sense to measure the indicators objectively and compare them against the world at large. What is required is a comparison with other employers in the same business, or at least employers operating with the same working conditions or in a similar environment.

Risk/Performance Model

2–06 The risk/performance model indicates not only the scope for improvement and savings, but also the mirror image of that. The model indicates the extent to which health and safety issues are likely to beset and perhaps overwhelm the business — not only in terms of cost but also of enforcement proceedings and court action, both criminal and civil. Whenever I advise new clients on matters of safety I always spend some time mentally fitting them into the risk/ performance model. This helps to give me some idea of the type and extent of the problems that are likely to be uncovered, and also the way in which the solutions to those problems may be viewed by the client. The four groups who make up the model are shown in Table 2, and are described below.

Table 2

GILTS	STEGOSAURUS
LION TAMERS	JOY RIDERS

Gilts

In the top left box are the Gilts. The good performers in low risk **2–07** sectors. This is the group with least scope but also least motivation to invest in further improvements to safety. Only a small minority of low risk employers fall into this category — most lack both the culture and the infrastructure necessary to ensure a good perform-ance. Those that do will generally share some common features, such as a well-organised, stable workforce and a strong management culture. Employers whose businesses bring them into close contact with the high risk sector and safety issues — consulting engineers and claims assessors, for example — are often Gilts.

Lion Tamers

Considering the potentially disagreeable consequences of the job, I **2–08** am told that mortality rates amongst lion tamers are extremely high. Apparently they can obtain mortgages and insurance cover! Hence the use of this label to describe high risk/high performance employ-ers. They exist in a dangerous environment, yet they are sensitive to it, trained to deal with it, and keep mishaps to a minimum. They respect the sources of danger and act accordingly.

Lion tamers, large or small, will have strong, well-organised man-agement systems. There will be a heavy emphasis on training and internal discipline, with discrete, professionally qualified safety and occupational health functions. As with Gilts, many Lion Tamers will themselves be in the business of safety, such as the police and rescue services. Constant exposure to the effects of injury reinforces their own safety culture. Others have reached this position after a bitter legacy of many years of high accident rates and ill health (for example, the coal mining industry, where the once widespread disease of pneumoconiosis was virtually eradicated by improved ventilation and dust suppression methods).

Although already successful managers of safety, Lion Tamers are always eager to develop their knowledge and to consider new ideas. I notice that they are invariably well represented at the safety seminars and conferences at which I speak, often asking questions and using coffee breaks as opportunities to informally compare notes with speakers and other delegates.

Stegosaurus

2–09   My experience has led me to believe that low risk organisations are mainly made up of (relatively) poor performers. I call these stegosaurus, after the dinosaur at the top of the food chain who nevertheless failed to adapt and so died out. No doubt the lack of history and experience of serious injury, or accidents on a significant scale, leads employers into complacency as regards the few material risks which *do* exist. Stegosaurus are often characterised by a poor understanding of their legal obligations as employers and a patchy (or non-existent) health and safety management system. Responsibility for safety often rests with the personnel director or the building manager. Sometimes departmental or line managers do not recognise any responsibility for the safety of their staff.

Stegosaurus have been affected more severely than most groups by the tightening up of legislation in recent years. Many have still not instituted risk assessment as required by the Management of Health and Safety at Work Regulations 1992 (see Appendix 7). The obligations towards display screen users to assess workstations, enforce breaks, and offer eyesight tests pass them by. When they do run foul of the enforcement authorities managers of stegosaurus are frequently surprised at the extent of the inspectors' powers and at their own vulnerability to prosecution and enforcement notices. Stegosaurus are also vulnerable to compensation claims. In particular from display screen users suffering from work related upper limb disorder and from more novel species of claim such as stress and passive smoking.

Joy Riders

The Joy Riders are the *really* dangerous employers — poor performers in a high risk business, taking unnecessary risks with their own and others' lives. This group has the most to gain by adopting a health and safety management system, and formulating and enforcing a sensible policy. Yet, paradioxically, Joy Riders are the group least likely to take that course of action: least likely to attend training courses and seminars. The fact that you are reading this book at all makes it unlikely that your organisation is a Joy Rider!   **2–10**

It may be unwise to generalise too much, as some joy riders exist in nearly all high risk sectors. Nevertheless I have observed a number of features which are often present in joy riding organisations. Amongst these are a widely dispersed workforce; a high turnover of staff; a reliance on temporary or contract workers; a preponderence of untrained or poorly trained school leavers; "self employed" sub-contractors; and a mobile or peripetetic workforce. Of course, a number of Lion Tamers and Gilts will also exhibit one of more of these features, but, in my experience, where four or five of these features come together in one organisation the chances of it being a Joy Rider are fairly strong.

There may be some movement from box to box, particularly from right to left, as Joy Riders seek to become Lion Tamers, and Stegosaurus Gilts. Unfortunately, there is sometimes movement in the opposite direction, perhaps as the result of a change of ownership or new management.   **2–11**

Although more rare, there may occasionally be movement up or down boxes. The introduction of new technology may reduce the inherent risks of the business, in some cases dramatically (*e.g.* development of electonic transfer to reduce movement of cash on a large scale). The most dangerous movement, however, occurs when a company diversifies from a low risk business into a high risk enterprise. Unless they take careful steps to buy in the necessary technical safety know-how, they may turn themselves into Joy Riders.

CHAPTER 3

SETTING UP A MANAGEMENT SYSTEM

The Systematic Approach

Health and safety management is not an arbitrary matter. It cannot **3–01**
be left to chance. Or rather, it can be left to chance but the chances
are that it will fall. Like many other aspects of life (*e.g.* selling, or
negotiating) safety management is a mechanistic process. It can be
learned; it can be improved by training; and it can be measured and
audited against pre-determined standards. That is to say, it can be
systemised — which is just as well, because the law requires that
management of health and safety be subjected to a systematic
approach. It may not *require* a system in so many words, but the
requirement is clearly implicit from the legislation. Consider the key
words of modern safety laws: policy, arrangements, assessments,
training, review. These only make sense within the context of an
overall system.

Key Duties

There are an extremely large number of specific legal requirements **3–02**
regulating workplace safety, running into many thousands. Of
course, not all of them apply equally to all employers. Many are
sector or process specific. Some are more onerous than others.

Formerly they were largely prescriptive, in that they laid down particular, objectively measurable standards. Since the Health and Safety at Work etc. Act 1974 (see Appendix 6), however, legal duties have been generalised — setting employers broad goals and leaving it to them to determine how best they are to be achieved.

The main duties introduced by the 1974 Act, which still hold sway today, include:

1. A duty on employers to ensure, so far as is reasonably practicable, the health and safety of employees.

2. A duty on employers to ensure, so far as is reasonably practicable, the health and safety of persons not employed by them but who may be affected by the employers' undertaking (or "business" in the broadest sense of the word).

3. A duty on occupiers of premises used for non-domestic purposes to ensure, so far as reasonably practicable, the health and safety of those who use those premises. For these purposes an "occupier" is someone who, to any extent, controls the premises in question.

It can be seen that these duties, few and simple though they are, are both wide-ranging and onerous. Indeed, in many respects, these goal-setting duties are more difficult to demonstrate compliance with than many of the pre-1974 detailed requirements. If objective and measurable standards have been achieved then the employer has not been in breach of duty, and that's that. Under the 1974 Act the reasoning may work the other way around. If an accident has occurred then sufficient care cannot have been taken (subject to the defence of reasonable practicability) for the safety of the injured person, and therefore the employer must be in breach of the Act. The standard set by the 1974 Act, therefore, presents a substantial challenge to employers.

Ingredients of the System

3–03 A number of the key constituent parts of any safety management system are covered in the next few chapters, including safety policies, risk assessments, audit and review. The Management of Health and Safety at Work Regulations 1992 (which are described in greater detail in Chapter 13 below and set out in full at Appendix 7) are central to all safety management systems. In order to ensure compliance with the Regulations the following issues need to be addressed in the system.

(i) Risk assessment—General assessments are required by all **3–04** employers as well as the self-employed, in order to determine what steps need to be taken to ensure compliance with statutory duties, in respect both of employees and others affected by the employer's business. Risk assessments are discussed in more detail in Chapter 6.

(ii) Health and safety arrangements relating to the planning, 3–05 organisation, control, monitoring, and review of the employer's safety measures—This obligation must be read in conjunction with the requirements of section 2(3) of the 1974 Act for a statement of the employer's health and safety policy, organisation and arrangements. See Chapter 5, Health and Safety Policy.

(iii) Appropriate health surveillance having regard to any risks 3–06 identified by the assessment—This provision is intended to prevent disease or occupational ill health. Many low risk occupations may require no surveillance at all, and where it is necessary it may vary from job to job. For example, those exposed to dust or fume may need periodic x-rays; those working in noise may need regular audiometric tests. The professional and service sectors do not escape the surveillance net, and there is a statutory duty to provide eyesight tests for users of display screen equipment.

(iv) Health and safety assistance—All employers must appoint one **3–07** or more competent persons to assist in undertaking the measures necessary for ensuring compliance with statutory duties. Hence, at least one person in the organisation must carry a formal appointment as a "competent person". The appointee may be internal or external and his competence may (particularly in non-technical or low risk enterprises) be derived from experience and an understanding of current best practice rather than formal qualifications. That is to say, the appointee does not necessarily have to be a health and safety professional.

The number of appointees will depend upon the size and complexity of the organisation. Generally, the fewer the better — "as many as necessary and as few as possible" is the golden rule. Too many appointees will get in each other's way, engage in "turf wars" and obscure lines of command. In some cases two appointees may be one too many!

3–08 **(v) Procedure for serious and imminent danger and danger areas**—The system should encompass procedures to be followed in emergencies and should include the nomination of sufficient people to assist in the evacuation of premises. Access to areas of particular danger should be restricted. See Chapter 9, disaster Planning, for a more detailed consideration of these issues.

3–09 **(vi) Information for employees**—The system must be able to deliver information to employees, in a relevant and comprehensible form, on a range of issues. These include risks identified in the assessment, the employer's protective and preventive measures, the "imminent danger procedures" described immediately above, the identity of those nominated to assist in evacuation procedures, and risks notified by other employers sharing the same workplace.

3–10 **(vii) Multi-employer workplaces**—There should be a place within the system for the co-ordination of compliance measures by employers sharing a workplace, and co-operation between those employers so as to enable each of them to comply with statutory duties. The host employer is responsible for providing safety related information to visiting employers (and in some circumstances direct to visiting employees). Chapter 8, Control of Contractors, examines this area in greater depth.

Choice of System

A number of separate management system models exist, and **3–11** employers will have to decide which system is right for them. Very large or highly complex employers will probably have the resources to develop systems which are customised to their specifications. For different reasons very small employers will find it simpler to develop a system that suits their unique needs. Most employers in between these two extremes will probably select a system from a number of existing models, possibly refining it to suit their own needs. A number of "off the peg" systems are available and there is certainly no shortage of consultants prepared to set up one for you. I nearly always advise clients to develop their own systems — although they may well benefit from external help in stimulating the thinking process or in refining and polishing up the final draft. Whilst it is not a formal management system, the Health and Safety Executive's publication HS(G)65 offers valuable guidance on the essentials of a systematic approach. Whatever health and safety management system is ultimately chosen, it *must* suit the needs of particular organisations. For many employers the greatest danger lies not in a system which is insufficiently developed, but in one which is too complex and burdensome. A management system that is overcomplicated is as bad as no system at all: there is a grave danger that the effort needed to satisfy the demands of the system will lead to unnecessary bureaucracy and detract from its effectiveness. One is reminded of the student who spent so long preparing the perfect revision timetable that he ran out of time to revise! Unless they are subjected to a firm dose of pragmatism management systems have a habit of running out of control and dominating, rather than serving, the needs of the business.

An important development in management systems occurred in **3–12** April 1996 with the publication of a British Standard in health and safety management: BS8800. All employers seeking to develop or modify their own systems should look closely at BS8800, whilst new employers setting up a system for the first time could do no better than to adopt it in its entirety.

BS8800, which is long overdue, has the merits of both simplicity and pragmatism. Its specific requirements are kept to a sensible minimum and it has optional sections depending upon whether employers wish to adopt a dedicated safety system or to integrate safety with the existing environmental management system ISO

14001. Unfortunately, BS8800 remains a guide to best practice: it is not yet possible for organisations to be assessed against its requirements and to receive accreditation for compliance. Almost all clients with whom I have discussed the matter are disappointed at their inability to obtain a badge of compliance with the new standard. It seems likely that if it is to survive in the long term as a useful management tool BS8800 will have to adopt a formal accreditation procedure.

Summary, Checklist and Legal Sources

3–13 There is an implicit obligation upon employers to manage health and safety in a systematic way.

1. Choose a system which suits *your* organisation.

2. Don't overcomplicate — KEEP IT SIMPLE!

3. Address these issues in the system (all references are to the Management of Health and Safety at Work Regulations 1992 and HSWA 1974):

   Risk Assessment — Regulation 3
   Policy S2(3) and Arrangements — Regulation 4
   Surveillance — Regulation 5
   Assistance — Regulation 6
   Emergency procedures — Regulation 7
   Information to employees — Regulation 8
   Multi-employer sites — Regulations 9 and 10

CHAPTER 4

THE MANAGEMENT STRUCTURE

At the heart of the health and safety system lies the management **4–01** structure. Almost every other aspect of health and safety manage- ment is dependent upon a sound, integrated structure. The management structure is the point of delivery of the safe system of work, the safe environment, and safe plant and equipment. Without the right structure for *your* organisation, failure of the health and safety system is inevitable.

Health and safety management is simply one aspect of overall quality management. It is that part of quality management which ensures, in a controlled and systematic way, both the safety of operations within the areas of production and quality control, as well as a safe product. It encompasses both the organisation's obligations towards its own employees and other workers on site as well as the safety of the end user of the product.

In a paper published in 1992 the Health and Safety Commission said this: "Public Inquiries into recent major disasters have identified failures of management structure as a major underlying cause of the incident. Even in the largest companies senior management has often failed to recognise and respond to its duties." A sound management structure is therefore a prerequisite for an effective safety system.

Structure? What Structure?

4–02   When I use the term "management structure" I mean just that — the way in which the management of the organisation is structured. *All* of the management. The *whole* of the organisation. I draw no distinction between general management and health and safety management. Each is an indivisible part of the other. At the risk of over-emphasising the point I sometimes tell clients that there is no such thing as good health and safety management — there is only *good management*. The fact is that it is almost unknown for an organisation to be well managed generally but, for some reason, to have a hopeless approach to safety. Normally the two aspects go hand in hand. Likewise, a poor approach to safety is a fairly reliable indicator of uncertain overall management.

This principle — of integrating health and safety management into the overall management structure — means that all managers must accept some degree of responsibility for safety within their general area of authority. The other side of this coin is that every member of the organisation whose role includes the management of safety is part of the management structure. This is so even though they may not fulfil roles traditionally thought of as part of "management" (*e.g.* front line supervisors).

The Seamless Web

4–03   The management structure should define, in a clear and concise way, what authority and responsibility each person within the structure (or each level within the structure of a larger more complex organisation) holds. The structure should reveal a seamless web of responsibility extending outwards and downwards from the Boardroom to the factory floor. At each descending layer of management the responsibilities of individuals become more specific — less concerned with policy and strategy and more concerned with operational management and supervision. The definition of individuals' responsibilities within the structure should include a statement of whom, or what classes of persons, the manager has authority to instruct and — just as important — who has authority to instruct *him*.

Ultimate responsibility for health and safety lies in the Boardroom, and one director should carry responsibility for health and safety performance at a corporate level. That person does not himself have to manage safety — but he does have to ensure that it is managed.

The Safety of Operations

In devising the management structure one guiding principle will be **4–04** that responsibility for operations or particular activities will normally carry with it responsibility for the safety of those operations and activities. Those who manage activities must accept that they have a responsibility for the safety of those activities. Health and safety is therefore a line management function. Those who carry management responsibility for, say, production must accept primary responsibility for those engaged in the production process. Similarly, those responsible for quality control must accept responsibility for the safety of those engaged in the quality control process. The same principle should apply even to low risk environments. For example, the Finance Director will have a duty to ensure that his secretary complies with the Display Screen Equipment Regulations 1992 (see Appendix 9). He may be entitled to rely on specialist advice to ensure that the dimensions of the workstation comply with the law, but only he can ensure the compliance of work practices — *e.g.* regular breaks from keyboard work. The Finance Director may express mild surprise at the proposition that he has line management responsibility for his secretary, as might other office-based managers. But they do. Not for ensuring that the secretary doesn't slip in the canteen or fall down the lift shaft, but for ensuring the safety of her work as a secretary. It is partly a failure by managers to recognise that responsibility which has led to an upsurge in work related upper limb disorder claims in recent years.

Common Pitfalls

One familiar area of failure of health and safety management and **4–05** practice lies in the interaction of maintenance or repair work and the production process. For example, breaches of legislation occur, with depressing regularity, where a machine operator and a maintenance fitter each thinks that the other has locked out, or isolated, an item of equipment. In fact, neither has done so, with the result that one or the other receives an unexpected electric shock or becomes caught up in moving parts.

The safeguard against failure in this area lies in well-defined structures and roles. There must be well-understood procedures for handing over particular machinery or processes to a maintenance technician and the handing back when servicing or repairs have been effected. The least confusion over roles and structures will inevitably lead to accidents.

The Safety Officer

4–06 What is the role of the safety manager, or site safety officer, and where does he fit within the management structure? Even though I have said that safety management is a line management function, there may well be a valuable role for a separate safety manager standing outside the production chain of command — particularly in large or complex organisations with a high level of technical compliance requirements. The safety manager may usefully monitor and advise on legislative requirements, and organise training and audits. He may organise forums, such as safety committee meetings, and liaise with the enforcement authorities. It should, however, be clearly understood that his role is advisory and does not carry executive authority. (The exception to this rule may be a "long stop" or residuary power to issue instructions in the case of imminent danger or in the absence of line managers.)

Summary and Checklist

4–07 An organisation's management structure should complement its general style, culture and the nature of the organisation itself. The structure of a complex multi-site organisation will be different from a single-site small to medium sized enterprise; the structure of a manufacturing company will differ from an employer in retail, or in the service sector. In each case, however, the starting point should be the way the organisation works and what it does — and the management structure will fit in around it. Devising an abstract structure and trying to fit the organisation around it is to be avoided.

Checklist:

1. Does the structure complement the organisation?

2. Does one senior manager or director carry the safety portfolio?

3. Does responsibility for safety management lie where it ought to — with line management?

4. Does everyone in the organisation understand who they are responsible for (apart from themselves) and who is responsible for them?

5. Is the division of responsibility between different roles, or classes of manager, clear?

CHAPTER 5

HEALTH AND SAFETY POLICY

It is a legal requirement for organisations to have in place a health **5–01** and safety policy. The word "policy" may be somewhat misleading. What is required in law is a statement of the employer's health and safety arrangements and organisation. (Where there are five or fewer employees the employer is exempt from this requirement.) It should include, in written down or diagrammatic form, the management structure discussed in Chapter 4.

The policy statement is fundamental to the United Kingdom's health and safety legal system. It is a centrepiece of legislative requirements and any failure to possess a policy, or an up to date policy, is regarded as a serious breach of the law. Nevertheless, a policy statement will not usually be a difficult document to draft or to keep current — although, of course, there may be exceptions where highly complex, diverse or specialist employers are concerned. For most employers what is needed is no more than a little thought, some planning and clarity of expression.

One area which the policy does need to deal with is the detailed organisation of health and safety within the enterprise, and the arrangements for securing safety. Many policies, whilst containing broad statements of commitment to safety, neglect the necessary detail. A number of Public Inquiries into major disasters have been critical of the tendency for safety policies to be too strong on "pious good intent" at the expense of the nuts and bolts of the policy.

Status Review and Planning

5–02   Before determining its policy an organisation will need to establish the current status of its organisation and arrangements. You will have a much better idea of how to get to your destination if you know where you are starting from! This initial status review will inform and direct the organisation's thinking on the issues which it will need to address in the policy statement.

Following the status review some forward planning needs to be done to map out the objectives which the organisation is to set itself. Where does it want to go? How is it going to get there? As part of this planning phase objectives need to be established, health and safety targets agreed with managers and supervisors and standards set. In carrying out this planning phase, two requirements are paramount: ensuring that all objectives and standards set are both *measurable* and *achievable*. If an objective cannot be measured then you will never know if you've achieved it; and if it is not achievable then there is no point in setting it in the first place.

Drafting the Policy

5–03   The first piece of advice which I give to any client who is formulating his health and safety policy is that it must be *his* policy. Like the management structure, it must complement the organisation — it must fit around the way the enterprise works and what the enterprise does. No two organisations are identical, and therefore no two policies will be identical, although many will share common features.

For this reason "off-the-shelf" policies are to be avoided. They bypass the essential thinking process which should inform, and distinguish, the policies of individual organisations. There is no short cut to a sound policy. You cannot buy it — you have to formulate it and write it!

Nevertheless, drafting a health and safety policy is usually well within the range of competence of managers within the organisation. There may be some employers whose areas of activity are so technically diverse or specialist that it is sensible to bring in outside help for the drafting process, There may be reasons of convenience for outsourcing drafting. But only rarely will it be *necessary* for the drafting of the policy to be undertaken outside the organisation.

The Structure of the Policy

Even though the substance of individual policies will display an   **5–04** infinite variety, it is useful to adopt a fairly standard format. There is a core of issues which almost all policies will need to address. An appropriate model for a health and safety policy may well be a core policy document supplemented by a number of satellite documents. The core policy sets out the organisation's general statements and intent. The satellite policies deal with specific issues such as emergency procedures, manual handling, display screen equipment and control of contractors.

This modular approach to safety policies enables managers to weight the overall policy in favour of the areas of greatest relevance to the particular organisation. It also enables individual satellite policies to be updated or replaced with minimal disruption and without the need to amend the core policy. The outline policy document at Appendix 1 sets out a modular structure for a health and safety policy and includes a checklist of issues which the policy will need to address.

Communication

However good the policy is, it will not be effective unless it is   **5–05** communicated to those whom it seeks to cover. This will certainly include employees but may also, depending upon the nature of the organisation, extend to contractors and their employees — and possibly also to members of the public. The policy, or relevant extracts from it, needs to be distributed. It is not enough for the policy to be freely available — it must be placed into peoples' hands.

The extent to which visitors should be familiar with the policy varies according to the nature and purpose of the visits. At one end of the spectrum casual visitors may need no more than brief information on evacuation procedures. Conversely, contractors who are permanently or intermittently on site will need to be as familiar with the policy as the organisation's own employees.

Review

5–06 Eventually, the policy has been formulated, drafted, and communicated. So, that's the end of the work on the policy, is it? Well, unfortunately, not quite. Once in place the policy must be kept under review and updated as necessary. Changes in legislation, different working practices and the introduction of new technology are all likely to require some modification to the policy. It is, for example, probable that the legislative changes in health and safety which have been implemented since 1993 will have prompted changes in many employers' safety policies.

Summary and Checklist

5–07　　1. Review the current status of health and safety management within the organisation.

2. Plan the steps that need to be taken and set objectives and standards.

3. Formulate the policy statement — the declaration of intent and the broad approach to health and safety.

4. Draft the detailed organisation and arrangements for securing health and safety.

5. Communicate the policy.

6. Review the policy.

7. Ensure the person, or people, responsible for the various stages of the policy are identified in the management structure.

Legal Sources

— Section 2(3), Health and Safety at Work — see Appendix 6 **5–08**
for full text.

— Regulation 4, Management of Health and Safety at Work
Regulations 1992 — see Appendix 7 for full text.

CHAPTER 6

RISK ASSESSMENT

Risk Assessment — What's It All About?

Of all the legal changes which have overtaken the world of health and **6–01** safety in recent years, none has created such a stir nor generated as much interest as the general obligation to carry out risk assessments — first introduced by the Management of Health and Safety at Work Regulations 1992, set out in full at Appendix 7. Of course, some health and safety practitioners will tell you that there's nothing new about risk assessments. "It's implicit in the general duties under the Health and Safety at Work Act", they say. "Assessing risk is a prerequisite for ensuring peoples' safety". And so it is, in a rough-and-ready informal sort of way — but to nothing like the extent now required to be formalised and documented.

Risk assessments are also "not new" in another, slightly different sense. Obligations to carry out specific risk assessments, intended to control the risk of particular substances or agents, have been in existence for many years. Exposure to asbestos, lead, noise and hazardous substances have all been subject to the requirement to perform suitable and sufficient or adequate risk assessments.

Yet the general duty ushered in by the 1992 Regulations on January 1, 1993 has been greeted with uncertainty and hesitation by many employers. Some have not yet completed their initial assessments, let alone kept them under review. Others have completed assessments, but in a way which seeks minimal compliance with legal requirements: the assessments may often be viewed as a bureaucratic chore and once completed they are filed away not to be looked at again until a formal review process begins.

Mention of risk assessments to many clients commonly produces **6–02** one of two distinct reactions. Either they concede, with a weary shrug of resignation, that the organisation hasn't really got on top of the assessment. Or, with a cry of triumph, they declare that all assessments have been finished and filed away ready to be seen, if required, by an H.S.E. inspector. Of the two the former reaction is the less unwelcome! Only a minority of employers seem genuinely to be comfortable with the duties and to comply in the manner envisaged by the 1992 Regulations and their supporting Approved Code of Practice.

The reason why many organisations have found it difficult to get to grips with the requirement to conduct general risk assessments is not, I think, hard to find. The general obligation to assess risk is at the heart of an approach to workplace safety which is fundamentally different from what has gone before. More than any other single piece of legislation risk assessments suggest a proactive approach to health and safety, which contrasts with a traditionally reactive philosophy to safety which has held sway since the beginnings of the Industrial Revolution. During that time, there have in particular industries been any number of success stories of declining accident rates and diseases being overcome. Many of these advances followed on directly from prescriptive legislation which was itself a reaction to major disasters or unacceptably high accident rates. The occurrence of serious harm was seen as a major agent of change — and in the absence of evidence of harm there was little motivation *to* change. In expecting employers to assess risks and to act on the basis of those assessments we are asking them to effect changes in the absence of any evidence of harm. We are challenging one of the basis tenets of management — "if it ain't broke don't fix it". It is not surprising that many employers have been slow to embrace this new philosophy.

The Nature of the Duty

6–03 Under Regulation 3 of the Management of Health and Safety at Work Regulations 1992 every employer is obliged to make a suitable and sufficient assessment of the risks to the health and safety of his employees to which they are exposed whilst they are at work as well as the risks to people not in his employment arising out of or in connection with the conduct of his undertaking. The purpose of the assessment is to identify the measures which the employer needs to take in order to comply with his statutory duties. Those who are self-employed are placed under a like duty.

Of course, before the risk can be assessed, the hazards have to be identified. This distinction, between hazard and risk, is fundamental to successful risk assessment.

— A hazard is something which has the potential to cause harm. It may arise from plant and equipment, systems of work or the work environment.

— A risk is the likelihood of a particular hazard actually causing harm together with the consequences for those affected by the hazard — *i.e.* the chances of serious injury or death.

Assessing risk therefore calls for a quantitative exercise of judgment. It is more than an exercise in identification. One of the common reasons for inadequate or incomplete risk assessments is a failure to keep in mind the difference between a hazard and a risk, leading to an unhelpful list of risks without any real effort to evaluate them.

As with some other aspects of occupational health and safety management, there is a perception that assessments are more difficult and demanding to carry out successfully than is in fact the case. However, many of the problems recede if employers concentrate on the key distinction between hazard and risk and avoid overcomplicating the process.

The format of the assessment is one issue which occasionally gives rise to unnecessary levels of concern. What does a risk assessment *look like* and how do you set about filling it in? Fortunately, the great majority of assessments can be completed in a simple format, which is illustrated at Appendix 2. When completed the assessment is best regarded as a set of action points — a blueprint for change. What it should *not* develop into is a set of documents to be deposited in a filing cabinet and forgotten.

Stages in Risk Assessment

Risk assessments are best approached in a sequential set of logical **6–04** stages, as dicussed below.

1. Classifying Activities

Question: How do you eat an elephant? Answer: In small chunks. Risk assessments are a bit like that.

Even in small to medium sized enterprises there will be a surprisingly high number of separate activities, or types of activities, carried on. They have to be broken down into manageable chunks and tackled separately. Remember, what are being assessed are risks, not individual employees. Similar physical activities or processes may be the subject of generic assessments.

It is at this stage that an employer can legitimately address the issues of trivial risks — those risks which involve very minor hazards, whose consequences are mild or which are unlikely to materialise anyway. The Approved Code of Practice supporting the MHSWR 1992 (Paragraph 9) makes it clear that trivial risks can usually be ignored. Of course, it is a matter of judgement as to which risks fall within this category. If in doubt, do *not* treat a risk as trivial.

The purpose of this preliminary "risk assessment" is to ensure that the assessment proper concentrates on real, significant risks and does not become bogged down in a morass of very minor risks which would serve only to obscure the genuine dangers rather than highlight them.

I know that in recommending that this weeding out process be carried out at the initial classification stage some will say that I'm ignoring my own advice. No sooner have I urged that assessments be tackled in a logical series of stages, than I start mixing up the stages! It is, however, vital that risk assessments do not become sidetracked into dealing with matters of no real importance, and the stage of classifying activities is a sensible time to carry out this exercise.

2. Identifying Hazards

6–05 The next stage is to identify and list the hazards which you can reasonably expect to cause harm in the conditions prevailing in your workplace. In particular:

1. Look at hazards which arise from the *work activity* itself. Do not rely on manuals, internal codes of practice or permit to work systems: actual practise may differ.

2. Look at hazards which arise from the way the work is carried out — not just at the equipment or hardware. I once came across a display screen equipment "risk assessment" which had been carried out overnight so as not to cause any excitement amongst the staff who worked on the equipment during the day. Although this approach allowed the dimensions and general conditions of the work stations and surrounding area to be checked, it was impossible to identify hazards arising from working practice.

Appendix 3 Part 1 sets out a list of common hazards which may act as a guideline for hazard identification. Part II contains a checklist of the classes of people who may be affected by hazards. It is important to differentiate between these classes, as a hazard which will not be relevant to, say, members of the public may affect maintenance or repair staff.

3. Determining the Risk

When activities have been classified and hazards identified, the next, **6–06** and crucial, stage of the exercise is the determination of risk. This is the core activity of the risk assessment and calls for a high degree of judgment.

There exist a variety of methods for assisting employers in estimating the level of risk. As risk is the *product* of the likelihood of a hazard causing harm and the severity of the consequences, many of those methods involve a mathematical approach to the estimate. Numerical values may be ascribed to both likelihood and severity, and by multiplying one value by the other a "risk factor" is arrived at. For example, if there is a high probability that a hazard will materialise it might attract a value of 4, on a scale of 1 to 5. If, however, the severity of its effects would be mild, then a value of 2 might be appropriate, again on a scale of 1 to 5. Thus the risk factor would be 8 (4 × 2) out of a maximum of 25 — *i.e.* a fairly moderate risk probably requiring some limited remedial action.

Although this method seems to be in regular use by employers I have reservations about it. The use of numerical values seems to me to introduce a spurious element of scientific precision to what is, in the end, a question of individual opinion, albeit (hopefully) informed opinion.

For most organisations a less sophisticated method of estimating risk would be just as effective whilst being less time consuming. A simpler three-category matrix without numerical values has strong appeal as is shown in Table 3. This is the model which is suggested in the British Standard of Health and Safety Management — BS 8800.

Table 3

	Slightly harmful	harmful	Extremely harmful
Highly unlikely	TRIVIAL RISK	TOLERABLE RISK	MODERATE RISK
Unlikely	TOLERABLE RISK	MODERATE RISK	SUBSTANTIAL RISK
Likely	MODERATE RISK	SUBSTANTIAL RISK	INTOLERABLE RISK

The advantage of this "risk level estimator" is that it divides up levels of risk into no more than five separate risk bands, narrowing the scope for debate over categorisation of likelihood and severity and producing results in a simple and digestible format.

4. Specifying Action

6–07   Having estimated the level of risk, the action points necessary to eliminate and control the risk now need to be specified. In order to do this properly we need to be clear on what each of the five risk bands means and what degree of action (if any) is likely to be necessitated by them. The parameters in Table 4 offer a useful guide, and again feature in BS 8800.

TABLE 3

Table 4

RISK LEVEL	ACTION AND TIMESCALE
TRIVIAL	No action is required and no documentary records need to be kept. In retrospect, the type of risk which might have been identified during the classification process.
TOLERABLE	No additional controls are required. Consideration may be given to a more cost–effective solution or improvement that imposes no additional cost burden. Monitoring is required to ensure that the controls are maintained.
MODERATE	Efforts should be made to reduce the risk, but the costs of prevention should be carefully measured and limited. Risk reduction should be implemented within a defined time period. Where the moderate risk is associated with extremely harmful consequences, further assessment may be necessary to establish more precisely the likelihood of harm as a basis for determining the need for improved control measures.
SUBSTANTIAL	Work shoulfd not be started until the risk has been reduced. Considerable resources may have to be allocated to reduce the risk. Where the risk involves work in progress, urgent action should be taken.
INTOLERABLE	Work should not be *started* or *continued* until the risk has beeen reduced. If it is not possible to reduce risk even with unlimited resources work has to remain prohibited.

On the basis of the actions and timescales set out above, the risk assessment form at Appendix 2 can be completed with the appropriate remedial steps required to be taken, and the period during which they need to be completed. Those steps may then be monitored to completion. Where the employer employs five or more employees then he must record both the significant findings of the assessment and any group of employees identified as being especially at risk.

5. Reviewing the Assessment

6–08 The legal requirement is for risk assessments to be reviewed and where necessary modified when they are no longer valid or where there has been significant change in the matters to which they relate (MHSWR 1992 Regulation 3(3)). Although no set intervals are laid down for review it is sensible to build formal periodic reviews into the system, if only to guard against a failure to review in the circumstances envisaged by the legislation.

The fact that a regular review is due to take place at some stage should not however be used as a positive reason for putting off reviews following changes in the workplace. The type of changes likely to generate a review of risk assessments are similar to those which will prompt a re-evaluation of the safety policy itself and include the introduction of different systems of work and new plant and equipment.

The Assessors

6–09 There are a number of different views on the question of who should carry out the risk assessments. Provided that the assessor is both competent and trained to carry out the assessment there are no right or wrong choices: it is a question of who is best for the particular assessments in *your* organisation. In very small enterprises with simple structures the senior manager or owner of the business is often the most appropriate person to assess. In larger, more complex organisations the task will often be split up amongst a number of people, perhaps with the overall exercise co-ordinated by the functional safety department.

There is much to be said for risk assessments being carried out by those employees whose jobs are the subject of the assessments. After all, they know the job better than anyone and should therefore be in a good position to make sound judgments about risks associated with the job and the necessary preventive action. Such assessments do, however, need to be viewed with special care, as there may be a tendency for some employees who are very familiar with a particular machine or process to become rather complacent and to fail to properly recognise hazards which an assessor bringing more perspective to the exercise would identify immediately as something requiring attention.

Summary and Checklist

Plan a risk assessment programme which is suitable and sufficient for **6–10** *your* organisation. Build into the plan an assessment format, record keeping and regular reviews. Identify and train the accessors. In particular:

1. Classify work activities

2. Don't overcomplicate the process; discount truly trivial risks at an early stage

3. Identify the *hazard*

4. Evaluate the *risks*

5. Plan and carry out necessary remedial action

Legal Sources

General risk assessment

— Management of Health and Safety at Work Regulations 1992 **6–11** Regulation 3 — see Appendix 7

Specific risk assessment

— The Control of Lead at Work Regulations 1980

— Control of Asbestos at Work Regulations 1987

— Noise at Work Regulations 1989

— Display Screen Equipment Regulations 1992 — see Appendix 9

— Manual Handling Operations Regulations 1992 — see Appendix 10

— Control of Substances Hazardous to Health Regulations 1994

CHAPTER 7

AUDIT AND REVIEW

Audit

Regular auditing of health and safety systems is vital to sustaining **7–01** those systems, together with the policies and performance. It is a regrettable but undeniable fact of life that all systems deteriorate over time. If it were possible to establish the perfect system today; by tomorrow it would begin its long descent into obsolescence. Slowly at first, almost imperceptively, but steadily. The world moves on. New work practices emerge, legislation is superseded, people change. Unless your systems move along with the rest of the world they will inevitably fall out of step with the demands of the law. Auditing is one of the ways to guard against this.

Although there is no explicit legal duty to audit, in practice it seems inconceivable that any enterprise could fulfil the wide range of legal duties placed upon it without auditing its safety performance. No senior manager would dream of trying to run a business without financial auditing. Health and safety auditing is just as important to the long-term success of the organisation.

Scope

In accordance with a general systematic approach to safety, an audit **7–02** system will check, against agreed and defined standards, both the performance of the safety management system — including the operation of the management structure and the policy — and the standards on the factory floor. It will also embrace the system for

41

setting up and implementing the risk assessment programme. Audits should be carried out at regular intervals and, of course, a flexible approach is quite acceptable in that different audits (possibly at varying intervals) may be appropriate for different processes or parts of the business.

The type of audit carried out varies from "desk-top" studies designed to check the performance of systems (*e.g.* timely reviews of risk assessments or policy) to full scale audits which measure workplace conditions against agreed or legal compliance standards. There must also be established effective channels of communication to ensure that the results of audits are reported to those with senior management responsibility. Appropriate follow-up procedures are also necessary to ensure that the results of audits are acted upon.

Independence and Competence

7–03 As with risk assessments, there are few intrinsically right or wrong ways to audit — the primary issue is to identify that which is right for *your* organisation. There are, however, two fundamental principles which must be observed, failing which the audit will be invalid. These are *independence* and *competence*.

An audit which is not independent is no audit at all. However, the term "independent" as applied to health and safety audits means an independence of mind rather than a separation from the organisation being audited. It does not necessarily mean that those carrying out the audit will be external, although in practice they often will be. The required element of independence may be achieved by arranging for separate departments or sites to audit each other. Certainly many clients report that a healthy spirit of rivalry ensures that internal audits are often carried out with a ferocious rigour! Alternatively, in larger organisations audits may be entrusted to the company's health and safety department or manager.

Remember that audits, whilst important management tools, can only act as a check that the system which you have adopted is being adhered to. They cannot verify that this is the appropriate system. Likewise, audits can do no more than measure performance against pre-set standards; they cannot determine whether those standards have been set at the right level. Evaluating systems and standards requires a review ...

Review

Some senior managers insist that their systems and policies are under **7–04** constant review. Sounds good — but I doubt it's true. Oh, they may monitor their safety performance; they may audit their systems — but they're not *constantly* reviewing their systems. If they were then they would hardly have time to manage any other aspects of the business.

A genuine review is a substantial undertaking and presupposes a willingness and an ability to change. In reality it is almost inconceivable that organisations of any size are in a position to generate constant change. A constant rate of change would, in any event, be unwelcome, generating confusion and obscuring clear lines of command.

Formal review of an organisation's health and safety system, structure and performance should be undertaken at set periods (although that is not to say that particular processes or sub-systems should not be reviewed following specific events such as accident investigations or recommendations on expert advice). It should be undertaken by senior management, with assistance from key line managers and the safety manager. The involvement of senior management is important for two reasons. Firstly, it displays a commitment to the project which is likely to generate interest and commitment further down the chain of command. Second, the review will probably culminate in the need for at least *some* decisions on change to be taken at a senior level. Having a senior manager, or managers, on board from the start makes it far more likely that the right decisions will be forthcoming quickly and without unnecessary delay, following the completion of the review.

The review should be preceded by a wide-ranging information **7–05** gathering exercise. Accident rates and ill-health statistics relating to the organisation, comparisons with other employers in the same sector, audit results and risk assessment results all need to be considered — as do the existing management structure and safety policy. Employees or employee representatives should be consulted. Other stakeholders may also be canvassed for their views, including contractors, suppliers and customers. Finally, the relevant enforcement agency (the HSE or the local authority Environmental Health Department as the case may be) should be invited into the consultation process, and its advice sought. The totality of this information — both hard facts and opinion — all go into the melting pot and provide the platform from which to drive the review forward.

If the information gathering exercise described above sounds onerous or heavy-handed, remember that the exercise (and indeed the whole review process) needs to be proportionate to the risks and the safety issues to be addressed. A small organisation with simple structures, or one operating in a low risk environment, will need to spend only a relatively short period of time preparing for and carrying through the review.

And after the review? Well, then the results and conclusions are fed back into the planning phase of the health and safety management system, informing future decisions on the policy and structure and helping to maintain continuous improvement in safety standards.

Summary and Checklist

7-06 *Audit:*

1. Decide on the scope and extent of your audit system.

2. Establish effective reporting and follow-up procedures.

3. Ensure independence of auditors.

4. Ensure competence of auditors.

Review:

1. Set the periods of the review and agree on its objectives.

2. Base the review on up-to-date information and informed opinion.

3. Feed the results of the review into the planning phase of the system.

Legal Source

7-07 Regulation 4(1) of the Management of Health and Safety at Work Regulations 1992 provides that amongst the arrangements to which an employer is obliged to give effect are appropriate arrangements for the review of preventive and protective measures. See Appendix 7 for the full text.

CHAPTER 8

CONTROL OF CONTRACTORS

The ability of an organisation to control the activities of its contactors **8–01** has acquired a new significance throughout the last decade of the twentieth century. As it has become increasingly clear that employers may be held legally responsible for the actions of their contractors, so more thought has been given to the division of legal liabilities between contractors and those who engage them. The law, in exploring contractor relationships, has been doing no more than tracking the way in which the labour market itself has developed. The increasing use of non-direct labour has probably been the most significant development in employment trends in recent years. Outsourcing, contractorisation, facilities management, consultancies — all these terms represent a move towards non-direct labour. Of course, contractors have always had a place in developed labour markets, but formerly they were generally engaged in order to carry out specialist work or work which was not part of the employer's core business. Well, contactors still are used for these purposes but, increasingly, they are also engaged to perform functions which were once considered part of the employer's core business. In an increasingly competitive world, organisations in all areas, as diverse as heavy industry and the service sector, are seeking to protect their margins by cutting their direct costs and bringing in external labour wherever possible.

Not so long ago I was discussing these trends in employment law with a business acquaintance. He expressed the view that one reason why so much work is outsourced is because employers wish to avoid the increasingly unpleasant consequences of breaches of health and safety legislation. I strongly disagreed. Many of my clients outsource, often in circumstances where they would not have done so 10 years ago. Other clients, contactors, benefit from this trend. However, the driving forces behind these developments are almost entirely economic. I don't know any clients who outsource simply in order to avoid criminal liabilities for breaches of legislation which they would otherwise incur. If employers *do* outsource for that reason then they are in for a nasty surprise. If anything, the law is moving in the opposite direction, with employers more likely to be held liable in respect of work carried out by contactors — either instead of or as well as those contactors.

The Changing Legal Landscape

8–02   Section 3 of the Health and Safety at Work Act 1974 (set out at Appendix 6) requires employers to conduct their undertaking so as to ensure, so far as is reasonably practicable, that non-employees are not exposed to risks to their health and safety. Case law has established that "undertaking" includes:

— The provision of services as well as goods

— The carrying on of industrial processes

— Trading and supplying/selling of goods to customers

One case of particular importance is *R. v. Associated Octel Limited [1994] 4 All E.R. 1051 C.A.* The defendants (Octel) owned and operated a chemical plant and engaged a firm of specialist contractors to carry out routine cleaning and repair work during the annual shut down period. The contractor adopted unsafe working practices and an accident occurred in which one of the contractor's employees was severely injured. Octel were convicted under section 3 of the 1974 Act.

Octel appealed and argued that:

— The maintenance work was under the control of the contractors, and therefore was not part of Octel's undertaking.

— The accident had occurred during the period when the plant was shut down. As Octel was not carrying out its core business of chemical processing, it was not carrying out its undertaking.

The Court rejected these arguments and said that "undertaking" would include any cleaning, repair and maintenance of plant, machinery or buildings which is necessary for carrying on an undertaking. It is immaterial whether this maintenance work is carried out by an employer or an independent contractor. An occupier cannot, therefore, claim that the independent contractor's work is not a part of the employer's undertaking. The only possible defence in this case is that the employer took all reasonably practicable steps to avoid the offence, by demonstrating that they took safety factors into account in appointing the contractors, and that risk assessments were exchanged.

The "Reasonably Practicable" Defence

"Reasonably practicable" is a qualification found in most health and safety legislation. Wherever a statutory duty is placed on someone to have regard to health and safety matters, the duty is often moderated by the term "so far as is reasonably practicable".   **8–03**

Most health and safety legislation in recent years has been implemented in the United Kingdom pursuant to E.C. Directives. As the concept of "reasonably practicability" is nowhere to be found in the directives, it is arguable that the United Kingdom has not fully complied with its legislative obligations.

"Reasonable practicability" is a balancing exercise in which the degree of risk is weighed against the cost of averting the risk. The cost may be calculated in financial or manpower terms. If the risk is so slight as to be insignificant in relation to the cost of preventing it, an employer can argue that compliance with the relevant statutory provisions is not reasonably practicable.

What is "reasonably practicable" depends on the level of knowledge and technology at the time an incident takes place — in other words, you cannot take precautions against a risk which current knowledge has not identified as even existing, nor can you take precautions which have not yet been developed.

Multi-Employer Sites

8–04 Whenever there is more than a single employer occupying one site then problems with communication and reporting become compounded. An employer or occupier may have to deal with a multi-employer site not only where there are contractors on site for specific one off work, but also where other employers regularly visit the site for routine purposes, *e.g.* delivery and collection. Health and safety management systems should recognise the need for well defined procedures for dealing with other employers, and the employees of other employers. The Management of Health and Safety at Work Regulations (set out at Appendix 7) specifically require:

1. Co-operation between different employers sharing the same work site;

2. Co-ordination by different employers sharing a work site in their health and safety systems;

3. Exchange of relevant information.

There will be a range of circumstances where employers will wish to see the health and safety policies and risk assessments of other employers visiting their site and where they will need to let those other employers see their own policy and assessments. Furthermore, as occupiers may in certain circumstances have legal liability for the actions of their contractors, the system for letting contracts or out-sourcing areas of work should include, as part of the selection criteria, the tenderers' health and safety performance and record.

8–05 Under the Management of Health and Safety at Work Regulations 1992 the following information should be provided:

1. To persons exposed to any serious and imminent danger — The nature of the hazard and of the steps taken or to be taken to protect them from it;

2. To employees — Comprehensible and relevant information on the risks to their health and safety identified by any risk assessment, the preventive and protective measures taken,

procedures to be followed in the event of serious or imminent danger, the identity of persons whose duty it is to implement those procedures, any information provided to the contractor, by the operator concerning risks to the employees of the contractor arising out of or in connection with the operator's undertaking or vice versa;

3. To other employers — Information compiled by one employer concerning the risks to the employees of another arising out of or in connection with the conduct by the first employer of his undertaking;

4. Where employees of a contractor are working within the operator's undertaking — Information on the measures taken by the operator to comply with relevant statutory provisions insofar as those requirements relate to the employees of the contractor;

5. Where employees of a contractor are working within the undertaking of an operation — Information and instructions to those employees regarding any risks to their health and safety arising out of the conduct by the operator of his undertaking including sufficient information to enable both the contractor and his employees to identify any person nominated by the operator to implement procedures to be followed in the event of serious and imminent danger.

Policies for Dealing with Contractors

An organisation's health and safety policy should deal with its **8–06** relationship with contractors. See the check list at Appendix 1 for the areas which the policy needs to cover. The detailed areas for consideration include:

1. In relation to each contract in the course of which contractors' employees work at the organisation's premises, the organisation should appoint a competent person (the contract co-ordinator) to ensure compliance with the policy and with legal obligations. The contract co-ordinator should be

authorised to give directions on behalf of the organisation to the contractor.

2. The contract co-ordinator must co-operate with the contractor so far as is necessary to enable the organisation to comply with all its statutory duties. He should also take all reasonable steps to co-ordinate the measures taken by the organisation with the measures taken by the contractor.

3. Prior to the commencement of the contract, the contract co-ordinator should provide the contractor with the following information and documents:

   (a) Risk assessments which relate to or which may affect work to be carried out under the contract

   (b) The organisation's health and safety policy

4. Again, prior to the commencement of the contract, the contract co-ordinator should obtain the following documents from the contractor:

   (a) The contractor's risk assessments relating to or affecting the work to be carried out under the contract

   (b) The contractor's health and safety policy

   (c) Any instructions, procedures, method statements, codes, rules, notes of guidance or other documents relating to or affecting the work to be carried out

   (d) Any other information or documents relating to risks to the health and safety of the contractor's employees, the organisation's employees or employees of any other employers working on the same site

5. The contract co-ordinator must have the authority to give such instructions to contractors' employees as are necessary, in his opinion to secure compliance with the organisation's statutory duty. Where he does give an instruction to a contractor's employee which conflicts with a previous instruction given by one of the contractor's managers then he should

inform the contractor of his instruction as soon as practicable.

Summary and Checklist

1. Is there an adequate system for ensuring that only con- **8–07** tractors who can demonstrate competence and an appropriate health and safety management system of their own are awarded contracts?

2. Have the contractors been specifically informed of all matters which might affect the safety of the work which they are to carry out which would not be apparent from the contract documentation, or from the contractor's inspection?

3. Have you included control of contractors within your health and safety policy? .

4. Has relevant documentation (*e.g.* policies, risk assessments) been exchanged?

5. Has a specific person been appointed to oversee the relationship with the contractor?

Legal Sources

Section 3(1) of the Health and Safety at Work etc. Act 1974 requires **8–08** that employers conduct their undertaking so as to ensure, so far as is reasonably practicable, that non-employees are not exposed to risks to their health and safety. See Appendix 6 for full text.

Regulation 9 of the Management of Health and Safety at Work Regulations 1992 requires that where two or more employers share a workplace then each employer shall co-operate with the others so far as is necessary to enable them to comply with their statutory duties and shall take all reasonable steps to co-ordinate the measures which he takes to comply with his duties with the measures taken by the other employers. See Appendix 7 for full text.

Regulation 10 of the Management of Health and Safety at Work Regulations 1992 requires every employer to ensure that the employer and any employees from an outside undertaking who are working in his undertaking is provided with comprehensible information on risks to health and safety and the measures taken by him to comply with statutory duties. See Appendix 7 for full text.

CHAPTER 9

DISASTER PLANNING

We All Need a Disaster Plan

Most of this book is concerned with the prevention of accidents and **9–01** ill-health, including disasters. But all employers should spend some time considering how they would react if they were involved in a disaster, and plan accordingly. All management systems should therefore anticipate their own failure and address those actions which need to be taken in the event of a disaster occurring. In keeping with a theme which is common throughout this book, the extent and detail of the disaster plan should be in proportion to the level of risk. At one extreme employers in high risk undertakings will have detailed plans, frequent revisions, dress rehearsals, and good links with the emergency services. At the other extreme low risk employers may require little more than emergency evacuation and business interruption procedures. Nevertheless, however simple a plan may be I am firmly of the view that we all need one — and that includes employers in the commercial, service and professional sectors. The scale of the disaster, when it strikes, may have no relevance to the risks of the job and may in fact have nothing to do with the job at all. You may be caught up in someone else's disaster — affected by fire, explosion or contamination arising elsewhere. You may be the victim of a terrorist attack.

Although the causes of disasters are usually sudden and unpredictable (or at least, unpredicted) certain kinds of industrial activities carry known risks and are subject to detailed legal requirements for emergency planning. These include chemical or nuclear hazards at fixed locations, where the consequences of disaster are largely foreseeable. The requirements for these detailed plans are contained in the Control of Industrial Major Accident Hazards Regulations 1984 and also in conditions attached to licences issued to nuclear installations. Railway and offshore legislation require emergency planning to be dealt with by employers operating in these sectors in their safety cases.

What Is a Disaster?

9–02   Before we write our disaster plan we had better try and establish what we mean by the term. Unfortunately, there is no universally accepted definition, although most people reckon they know one when they see it. Emergency procedures manuals produced by the Fire Service and by the Association of Chief Police Officers define a major incident as any emergency that requires the implementation of special arrangements by one or more of the emergency services for:

1. The initial treatment, rescue and transport of a large number of casualties;

2. The involvement either directly or indirectly of large numbers of people;

3. The handling of a large number of enquiries from the public and media;

4. The large scale combined resources of all three emergency services;

5. The need to cater for the threat of death, serious injury or homelessness to a large number of people.

It seems fairly obvious from this definition that events which may well be viewed as disasters by organisations affected by them would nevertheless not be classed as major incidents by the emergency services. I usually advise clients that, in considering the point at which their emergency plans are triggered, a good working definition of a disaster *for them* is any event causing or threatening death or injury, damage to property, or interruption of business which, because of its scale requires the intervention of the emergency services and which cannot be dealt with by the employer concerned as part of his day to day activities. This definition enables organisations to gear their emergency plans to situations which are of particular relevance to them.

What Should the Plan Include?

There are a number of issues which should be common to all disaster plans — however simple the plan and however low risk the working environment. The extent to which the plan addresses particular issues will depend upon the needs of the particular organisation. My eight points for a basic disaster plan are the following: **9–03**

(i) Information Base

You must have a core information base of personal details regarding permanent staff and permanent contractors' employees on site (*e.g.* cleaners, caterers, security and maintenance staff). This should include names, addresses, home telephone numbers and details of relatives to be contacted in the event of injury. An efficient system also needs to be established for booking people in and out of the premises, where this is practicable (which it may not be for some organisations, *e.g.* the retail, leisure, sport and arts sectors). Wherever possible the aim should be to have an accurate record of the numbers and identity of those on the premises when the emergency arose.

At the risk of stating the obvious, duplicate personal details of staff need to be retained off-site and be easily and quickly accessible.

(ii) Liaison with Emergency Services

There's more to liaising with the emergency services than dialling 999. If you do ever have to rely on the emergency services it may be useful to know where your local accident and emergency unit is situated, where the fire and ambulance services are travelling from, **9–04** and at which station any police "incident control point" will be situated. In the rescue and aftermath phases telephone numbers and contact names of officials and officers will be important.

(iii) Emergency Procedures

Under the Management of Health and Safety at Work Regulations 1992 (regulation 7) employers must establish procedures to be followed in the event of serious or imminent danger; nominate sufficient people to implement those procedures insofar as they relate to evacuation from premises; and restrict access to dangerous areas. The procedures should also enable staff to leave work immediately and proceed to a place of safety and prevent them (save in exceptional circumstances) from resuming work where there is still a serious and imminent danger.

(iv) Command and Control

9–05 Who, within the organisation, is going to implement the plan? This should be determined beforehand and not left to chance on the day. Once the plan is in force structures must come into play to handle internal communication within medium or large multi-site organisations and generally to organise and oversee the carrying out of the disaster plan. Unless the organisation is unusually large or technically specialised this will *not* include rescue operations, which will be largely in the hands of the emergency services.

(v) Enforcement Agencies

As soon as the rescue phase, if any, is over and the aftermath phase begins the enforcement agencies, including the responsible inspectorate (usually either the Health and Safety Executive or the Environmental Health Department of the local authority) and the police, acting on behalf of the Coroner (where fatalities have occurred) will begin their detailed investigations. A senior manager within the organisation should be nominated to liaise and co-operate with these agencies. This will include ensuring that formal reporting procedures are adhered to and the provision of statements to the investigating inspector. This latter point is especially important, as these statements will often form the basis of subsequent legal proceedings.

(vi) Media Relations

Most clients think that devoting time to satisfying the demands of the **9–06** media is of trivial concern compared with the life and death issues surrounding emergencies and disasters. To the extent that media relations interfered with or detracted from rescue operations then those clients would be right. However, provided that this is not the case hard-headed clients realise that the media are going to write or say something, come what may, so you may as well tell them what you can in a clear and concise way.

Without being defensive care must be taken not to prejudice the legal position of the organisation (or of senior managers within it) by admitting allegations which may not be well founded or accepting facts as true which are still under investigation. In the initial aftermath of the incident it will usually be advisable to make it clear that the organisation is co-operating fully with the investigations and will offer every possible assistance to the investigating authorities. If it is premature to comment on possible causes (which it often will be) then this point should be stressed. My experience leads me to conclude that the operations manager most closely associated with the emergency is not always best placed to deal with media enquiries.

(vii) Business Interruption

Disasters interrupt business. That's a fact of life. So far as industrial fixed site specialised employers are concerned, there is little more to be said. If your plant is out of action then, generally speaking, it is simply not possible to move down the road and resume operations elsewhere. However, provided that adequate plans have been laid

57

beforehand, employers in the service and professional sectors often *can* move into empty office space and recommence business within 24 to 48 hours of bomb or other damage. Of course, the space has to be available, but cheap surplus office space *is* likely to be available well into the twenty-first century. Provision also has to be made for the downloading and remote storage of file data. But, with the right level of organisation these things can be, and have been accomplished. Often rival firms (preferably situated some distance from each other) will enter into mutual agreements to provide cover and telephone message facilities for each other.

(viii) Documentation

9–07   Needless to say the disaster plan needs to be documented. This is so even in the smallest and most low risk of enterprises. The perfect plan, ensconced in the head of the owner of a business, does no good if he is one of the victims of the disaster. Also, because the plan will rarely (if ever) be put into operation it will spend long periods of time gathering dust in someone's drawer. Whilst the plan remains the same the rest of the world moves on — managers come and go. When an emergency does occur the manager expected to deal with it may be oblivious to the very existence of the plan, let alone be familiar with its contents! For this reason the management system should provide for the re-appraisal of the plan annually, or upon a fresh appointment of a person charged with implementing the plan, whichever is the sooner.

Finally, the plan should be as simple and concise as possible. The shorter the better! A client once showed me an emergency plan which consisted of almost 1,000 pages of densely typed text, diagrams and appendices. The original authors had long since left the organisation. Not surprisingly no one else had managed to summon up the stamina to read the document.

Summary and Checklist

9–08   1. All organisations should possess a plan which regulates their responses to a disaster.

2. The plan should be proportionate to the risks and the complexity of the organisation.

3. Organisations should define what constitutes a "disaster" for them.

4. Plans should cover eight key points:

    —information base
    —emergency services
    —emergency procedures
    —command and control
    —enforcement agencies
    —media relations
    —business interruption
    —documentation

Legal Sources

— Control of Industrial Major Accident Hazards Regulations **9–09**
1984.

— Management of Health and Safety at Work Regulations 1992, Regulation 7, Emergency Procedures. See Appendix 7 for full text.

CHAPTER 10

LIABILITY — CRIMINAL

Introduction

From time to time most people find the law confusing and difficult to **10–01** understand. Sometimes even lawyers don't understand it, so it's not surprising that other people have trouble following its contours. As the criminal law has made greater in-roads into the relationship between employer and employee, one enduring area of puzzlement (I have found) has lain in the area of applying criminal standards to occupational health and safety.

Most directors and senior managers reckon they know what crime is, and what criminals are. When, though, dealing with breaches of legislation for which they may be responsible, or partly responsible, they do seem to have difficulty picturing themselves in the role of criminal. The "white collar" criminal is not at home in Court, and you can nearly always spot him or her. Waiting for cases to come on, they don't indulge in the good-natured joshing of the lawyers. Yet they look uncomfortable amongst the jeans and t-shirts of the more traditional criminal classes.

Many managers are, of course, familiar with the civil law — claims for compensation from injured or sick workers or former workers. And although the same accident can give rise to both criminal and civil proceedings, that's where the similarity ends. In terms of format, substance and outcome, a prosecution arising from an accident at work has more in common with car theft or breach of the peace than with a county court action for damages in connection with the same accident.

A crime is a crime, no matter who commits it and no matter what the offence. Table 5 sets out some of the main differences between crimes and civil proceedings.

Table 5

	Criminal	**Civil**
1. Nature of proceedings	An offence against the state where the state prosecutes the offender.	A private dispute between individuals or organisations.
2. Venue	Magistrates' Court for lesser or summary offences: Crown Court trial before a jury for serious offences.	County court for minor claims. High Court for high value or complex claims.
3. Standard of proof	Must be proved "beyond reasonable doubt".	Need only be proved "on balance of probabilities", *i.e.* more likely than not.
4. Outcome	Conviction if guilty. Acquittal if innocent.	Judgment for Plaintiff if claim successful. Judgment for Defendant if fails.
5. Consequence	Sentence: fine, imprisonment, probation, community service.	Court Order: damages, injunction.

This is a general indication of broad divisions of the criminal and civil law. In most categories there are some exceptions at the margins.

In looking at the operation of the criminal law in the field of health and safety it is probably useful to break down the discussion into two parts: corporate liability (where an organisation as a whole such as a local authority or a limited company commits an offence), and individual or personal liability.

Corporate Liability

Generally

Corporate liability — the legal liability of a corporate body, separate **10–02**
and apart from the individuals which make up that body — is a
relatively modern concept in English law. A body corporate itself is
best thought of as an artificial personality. The most common example of corporate bodies in the United Kingdom are limited
companies. Local authorities are corporate bodies, as are nationalised industries and some "quangos" (*e.g.* Development
Corporations). Boards of school governors recently acquired corporate status. Partnerships are *not* corporate bodies, each member of
the partnership being jointly and severally liable with his or her co-
partners.

Corporate bodies enjoy a legal status which is separate and apart
from that of the individual members or owners who make up that
body. Therefore, as they are legal personalities in their own right,
corporate bodies can do most things which real people can do —
including making contracts, suing, being sued and, of course, committing a criminal offence. However, as it is impossible to physically
imprison a corporate body any punishment in a criminal case will
normally take the form of a fine.

Breaches of Health and Safety Legislation

There are several dozen Acts of Parliament (some of which are **10–03**
industry or sector specific) regulating safety; several hundreds sets of
regulations; all of which give rise to thousands of separate duties,
requirements, and restrictions. Breach of any of these may amount to
a criminal offence and result in a conviction of the "person":
"employer"; "occupier" or "owner" (all of which terms include a
corporate body) upon whom the particular legal obligation is placed.
In practice however, apart from highly specialised occupations or
unusual accidents, the great majority of criminal prosecutions are
founded upon relatively few statutory duties. Although precise statistics are difficult to establish, it is probably the case that 5 per cent

of all statutory duties and restrictions account for over 90 per cent of all prosecutions. Furthermore, as few as three duties may account for as many as 50 per cent of all cases. These are the duties set out in sections 2, 3 and 4 of the Health and Safety at Work etc. Act 1974. These are summarised in Chapter 3 and set out in full at Appendix 6, but it may be recalled that they regulate, in turn, the general duties of an employer to his own employees; an employer to non-employees who are affected by his undertaking; and an occupier who controls non-domestic premises.

Some legal duties (and particularly the major general duties under HSWA 1974) require no proof of negligence or intent in order to secure a conviction. It is enough that the physical ingredients of the offence are present, and the mental failings, if any, of the corporate bodies or the officers or employees through which its acts are irrelevant. In relation to corporate liability generally the following points should also be noted.

10–04 An accident is not a prerequisite for a prosecution—Although prosecutions may follow accidents or injuries they are not limited to circumstances where these have occurred. General failures of the health and safety system may lead directly to criminal offences and thus prosecutions, including failures in the health and safety policy, training, supervision and risk assessment.

10–05 An offence is not a prerequisite for a Prohibition Notice—The test for a Prohibition Notice is whether the activity in question is one which involves, or will involve, a risk of serious personal injury. It is not necessary to prove that an offence has occurred in order for an Inspector to issue and sustain a Prohibition Notice.

10–06 A corporate body can be guilty of an offence through the actions of a junior employee—Although at a senior management level a corporate body may have established an appropriate health and safety management system, including training and supervision, that body may still be guilty of an offence where one of its junior managers, or one of its other employees, has committed a negligent act or a breach of statutory duty which causes or contributes to an injury. This may be so even where senior management could not reasonably foresee the act complained of. This principle has been clarified by the Court of Appeal in the case of *R. v. British Steel* ([1995] 1 W.L.R. 1356). Effectively it imports into considerations of criminal law the concept of vicarious liability, in much the same way that that concept has been effective for many years in the area of civil claims.

A corporate body may be guilty of an offence by virtue of the actions   10–07
of its independent contractor—There are a limited number of circumstances in which employers or occupiers may be guilty of an offence as a result of acts or omissions on the part of an independent contractor. The most recent example of this principle was the ruling by the Court of Appeal in *R. v. Associated Octel Limited* ([1994] 4 All E.R. 1051 C.A.) (see Chapter 8). In that case Octel were found guilty of a breach of section 3 of the Health and Safety at Work Act 1974 on the basis that its contractors had been working in Octel's "undertaking". This was so even though Octel exercised no control over the manner in which its contractors carried out their work, and where the contractors had been engaged on the basis that they were experts in their particular field. This case has established a wide definition of the term "undertaking" as used in health and safety legislation.

In addition to breaches of legislation, where there has been a fatal accident then in some, very rare circumstances a corporate body may be convicted of the common law crime of manslaughter. See Chapter 18 for a more detailed discussion.

Individual Liability

Generally

Although much less common than convictions of corporate bodies,   10–08
successful prosecutions of individuals are rather less uncommon that was formerly the case. Enforcement authorities have taken a more aggressive line in recent years. As one HSE inspector remarked to me, in terms of publicity and effectiveness "one conviction of a director is worth 10 convictions of a company". By and large, prosecutors have been pushing at an open door, with the judiciary (particularly at the senior, high court level) prepared to hand down prison sentences in serious cases. A handful of high-profile cases

attract a disproportionate amount of attention. Examples include the prison sentences imposed upon individual directors, managers or owners following the Lyme Bay canoeing tragedy in which four teenagers drowned (*R. v. Kyte* (*Health and Safety Bulletin* 229, January 1995)); the sinking of the trawler Pescado with the loss of all hands (*R. v. Parker* (*Health and Safety Bulletin* 244, April 1996)); and an asbestos contamination during a demolition project (*R. v. Hill* (*Health and Safety Bulletin* 243, March 1996)).

These few cases, indicative though they are, should not obscure the fact that only a tiny fraction of industrial accidents result in prosecutions at all; and of those that do the vast majority feature corporate bodies, not individual managers and directors.

In addition to manslaughter (in relation to which see Chapter 18) the main routes by which managers and other employees may incur liability are set out below.

Health and Safety at Work etc. Act 1974

Directors, Company Secretaries and Other Senior Managers

10–09 Section 37 of the HSWA is a key provision in relation to the personal liability of senior managers for work related accidents. It is set out in full at Appendix 6 and provides that *where* an offence has been committed by a body corporate *and* where that offence has been committed with the consent, connivance, or neglect of certain classes of individuals then those individuals will be guilty of the same offence. The relevant classes of individuals are any director; the company secretary; any other similar officer; any manager; or anyone purporting to act as any of the above.

The first point to note is that liability will only attach to these individuals where the company itself has been guilty of an offence. It is not, therefore, possible for a prosecution under this section to succeed against an individual in circumstances where the company is not guilty.

The second point to note is that an individual will only be guilty of an offence where he has contributed to the company's guilt by any "consent, connivance or neglect" of his own. Therefore, the extent to which an individual may be liable would depend upon the extent of the participation of that individual in the act which is complained of, the personal level of responsibility and the capacity in which he or she has acted. So far as directors are concerned, their liability will be determined by the level of their participation and by their particular responsibilities. A director who has actively participated in a decision and who carried particular health and safety responsibilities would be more likely to incur personal liability than a director whose level of participation was low and who did not carry any specific responsibility. No individual will be guilty purely by virtue of the position which he or she held. There must be some personal failing — either something which that individual did which should not have been done, or something which the individual failed to do which should have been done.

Whilst the positions of directors and company secretaries are fairly clear under the terms of the section, it is not similarly clear to what extent individual managers will be liable. How far down the chain of command does liability extend under section 37? This question has been examined in detail in several cases, including the case of *R. v. Boal* ([1992] 3 All E.R. 177), which was concerned with an identically worded section under the Fire Precautions Act 1971. Boal was an assistant manager of a retail bookshop. In that case it was held that a manager (who is not a member of the board) will only be liable for a criminal offence under section 37 if it can be shown that he or she was of sufficient seniority so as to be considered part of the corporate body's "directing mind", or part of the brain of the company as opposed to its hands or arms. In order to secure a conviction it would be necessary for the prosecution to prove that the manager concerned was responsible for general policy and strategy, and not simply day to day management, and that he or she participated in the management of the company as a whole. This definition would exclude most managers from the ambit of section 37 (and indeed Boal himself was found not to be sufficiently senior to fall within section 37).

Other Employees

Under section 7 of the HSWA (see Appendix 6) all employees are placed under a duty to take reasonable care to avoid placing either themselves or others who may be affected by their actions at risk. As it applies to all employees this section will, of course, catch junior or middle managers who may escape liability under section 37. Furthermore, prosecution under section 7 (unlike section 37) does not depend upon the corporate employer of the employee concerned **10–10** being guilty of an offence. In one case — (*R. v. LLewellyn-Jones* (*Health and Safety Information Bulletin* 211, July 1993) Section 7 was used to prosecute a college lecturer in whose laboratory several explosions occurred. The section has also been used to prosecute individual workmen — for example, for refusal to wear hearing protection.

Individual Owners

10–11 Individual (as opposed to corporate) business owners may also incur personal liability under HSWA. As such persons will be "employers" or persons who occupy and control premises, they may be liable under sections 2, 3 or 4 of the HSWA in respect of their own émployees, persons not employed by them or persons using their premises. In *R. v. Hill* (*Health and Safety Bulletin* 243, March 1996) an individual employer became the first person to incur an immediate prison sentence for a breach of health and safety legislation.

Management of Health and Safety at Work Regulations 1992

10–12 Under Regulation 6 of these regulations (set out at Appendix 7) employers are obliged to appoint a person to assist them to discharge their health and safety obligations. Depending upon the terms of the appointment the appointee may be prosecutable in relation to health and safety failures. It is, however, possible to draft an appointment which whilst fulfilling the statutory criteria, nevertheless limits the appointee's role to providing advice to the employer without any operational or executive authority. In such a case (provided of course that the advice is sound) the chances of a successful prosecution against the appointee are considerably lessened.

Disqualification of Directors

10–13 Under the Company Directors Disqualification Act 1986 directors of companies may be disqualified in certain circumstances. In the case of *R. v. Chapman* (*Health and Safety Information Bulletin* 200, August 1992) it was held that the circumstances included breaches of environmental, health and safety legislation by the company concerned. Since that case, there has been a steady increase in the number of directors disqualified for breaches of prohibition notices.

Miscellaneous Points

Insurance is of limited value in criminal cases. Employers' liability **10–14** and public liability policies will only cover the legal costs of defending the claim. The policy will not cover any fine imposed as a result of a conviction. Neither will an employers' and public liability policy extend to the costs of defending a prosecution against an individual director or manager, although Directors and Officers policies may cover such costs.

The fact that the injured workman may have contributed to his accident by neglect for his own safety is not, in itself, a defence to an allegation against his employer. Unlike civil claims for damages (where an employer's liability may be reduced in proportion to the plaintiff's "contributory negligence") in criminal law a defendant is either guilty or not guilty — he cannot be 50 per cent guilty or 75 per cent guilty.

What is the employer's position where there has been a breach of the terms of an Approved Code of Practice (ACOP)? The text of an ACOP is not part of the legislation and breach is not, therefore, in itself an offence. However, the fact of a departure from the terms of an ACOP may be used as evidence of a breach of statutory duty. It is open to a defendant to demonstrate that he has complied with the statutory duty by other means that are equally as effective as the requirements of the ACOP. Breach of an ACOP may also prompt other enforcement action such as an Improvement Notice or, in exceptional cases, a Prohibition Notice.

CHAPTER 11

LIABILITY — CIVIL

To Settle or Not to Settle?

"You'll settle this claim over my dead body".

    "It's a try-on — we'll see him in court".

    "He's no more deaf than I am — deny liability."

A few of the more polite remarks likely to greet the solicitor acting on behalf of an insurance company who has delivered to an employer — the insured — the advice that the works manager or chief executive did not want to hear: you're going to lose this claim — better to try and negotiate a good settlement out of court than to take the case through to trial.

Employers hate settling claims, understandably so. Managers may take allegations personally (as indeed they well might — many cases turn on allegations of personal failings on the part of individual managers or supervisors).

Finance directors see the increasing costs of the employers' liability premiums and want to exert pressure to keep the numbers of claims down. All agree that settlement encourages an escalation in similar claims — particularly where claims relate to occupational ill-health. Again, they may well be right.

And yet in the legal environment in which personal injury claims exist it is a fact of life that the great majority of claims will succeed — either out-of-court settlements will be obtained or the plaintiff will obtain judgment if the case proceeds to trial.

Different people will have their own views on whether this is a good or a bad thing, but setting opinions to one side, it is a factor which should inform the thinking of all those charged with the defence of injury or ill-health claims. The trick is to pick out the relatively few winnable claims at an early stage and contest them through to trial as quickly and cost effectively as possible. There may be some sound strategic or policy reasons for contesting claims, or large groups of similar claims, which are almost bound to succeed at trial. Possibly an employer or insurer will want to avoid creating the impression, in the minds of opposition lawyers, that they are a soft touch for claims, or claims may be resisted as a matter of negotiating strategy, in order to lay the ground for a broadly based scheme designed to turn over the claims quickly on the basis of set tariffs at minimal legal costs. Generally, though, cases that cannot be properly defended should be disposed of speedily and at minimal cost.

The Forces Shaping the Law

11–02 It is a common experience for most of us that, in our personal lives, we find insurance companies to be tough negotiators, and so far from being a "push-over" as can be imagined. Ever tried claiming on that house contents policy? What about a third-party claim against the other driver following a traffic accident? We usually have to work hard to substantiate our claim and we hardly ever recover the full amount. Yet, put an insurance claims manager in charge of an employers' liability claim and, in the view of many employers, he immediately begins to hand out money to claimants with unrestrained gusto.

The truth is that insurers are just as hard-nosed in dealing with employers' liability cases as they are with every other sort of claim. What they do have is a far better grasp of the realities of how the civil justice system works in the United Kingdom. Not just the strict requirements of the law, precedents, and the financial value of particular injuries or conditions, but a close working knowledge of the legal and social attitudes that underpin developments in personal injury litigation.

The main driving forces which have shaped the development of the law in this area include judicial attitudes and the interests of the legal profession.

Judicial Attitudes

"I regard it as part of my job to ensure that, when an injured **11–03** workman comes before my court, he leaves with some money in his back pocket." A remark, overheard, and made by a judge from a northern industrial city. The judge in question is certainly keen on doing what he perceives to be his job to the very best of his ability!

Judicial attitudes change over time. They reflect, in some measure, broad changes in the social and political attitudes of the rest of society. At the end of the twentieth century we have a liberally minded judiciary in the United Kingdom. On the whole, in less than a hundred years a powerful body of professional men have covered a lot of ground. From being widely regarded as a tool of repression they are now more likely to be viewed as champions of the rights of individuals against large institutions. This trend can most clearly be seen in the development of Judicial Review as a means of protecting citizens against an over-mighty executive. The quashing of decisions of government ministers by judges has become routine.

The effect of a liberal judiciary can also be seen in the development of civil claims for damages from workers who have been injured at work or who have developed a form of occupational ill-health. At Appendix 4 there is a selection of quotations from judgments in a number of civil personal injury claims. All the claims relate to industrial deafness, but the approach which they exemplify is fairly well representative. In each case the judge is assessing the credibility of the individual plaintiff — making an assessment of how much reliability can be attributed to his evidence. It can, I think, be concluded that these judgments betray a certain lack of healthy scepticism. They illustrate a mindset which is predisposed towards a rather unquestioning acceptance of the evidence of those who have a strong vested interest in the outcome of a claim.

The Legal Profession

Speaking of vested interests brings me quickly to the legal profession, **11–04** which has been a major engine driving forward damages claims in recent years — particularly the solicitors branch of the profession, and particularly claims for industrial diseases.

The vested interest here is not so much in the outcome of a case, because the lawyers get paid whoever wins the case, but in generating claims in the first place. (Although the recent introduction of "conditional fees" under which arrangements lawyers may obtain a portion of any damages awarded whilst bearing their own costs of any unsuccessful claim, has brought an element of vested interest into the outcome of claims.)

Freedom to advertise, since being extended to solicitors, has resulted in an enormous stimulation of the claims "market" as potential claimants have been encouraged to step forward. Although some of the ensuing claims have resulted in substantial compensation, many are settled for trivial amounts and it is not unusual for the legal costs of one side to the dispute — let alone the combined legal costs — to dwarf the amount of damages received by the plaintiff. The great majority of these claims are funded initially by the taxpayer through the legal aid scheme. Of course, the ultimate cost of settled claims or those which succeed at trial are borne by insurance companies often caught in the "legal aid trap", where it may cost them more to defend a claim (even if the defence succeeds) than to settle it cheaply at an early stage.

Insurance

11–05 Not so long ago the position with regard to insurance in compensation claims was pretty straightforward. You paid your premium, the insurer indemnified you against the claims, and that was that. In recent times, though, a number of factors have combined to unsettle the market and to challenge traditional relationships between insurer and insured.

E.L. Caps—A minimum level of £2 million employers' liability insurance in respect of any one incident is compulsory. Until recently, however, the market offered unlimited cover. This was replaced, for new policies written after 1995, by a cap of £10 million on cover. Although this is still comfortably above the minimum level, it does demonstrate the nervousness with which insurers now view the E.L. market.

Changing Labour Market—The employer/employee relationship is being increasingly replaced by outsourcing and use of contractors (see Chapter 8). Claims from employees of other employers will normally fall to be dealt with under a public liability policy, not an employers' liability policy. As it is not compulsory for employers to insure against their public liabilities, such claims may fall to be dealt with by the employer direct if the risk is uninsured, or underinsured. If the employer is insolvent, the plaintiff may be unable to recover his damages at all.

Industrial Diseases—The emergence of industrial diseases as a major source of claims (and especially asbestos and industrial deafness claims) has required investigations into plaintiffs' working histories extending back 20, 30 or sometimes 40 years. It is not uncommon for an employer to be simply unable to identify the insurer who was on risk at the time the relevant exposure took place. Once again this results in the employer dealing with the claims himself and, if he is insolvent or wound up then claimants may be unable to recover at all. Of course, it may be that funding claims direct makes a major contribution to that very insolvency, which results in an invidious position whereby some plaintiffs may have their claims met whilst others do not.

In addition, there are a number of rogue employers who fail to take out the compulsory minimum employers' liability cover. They risk prosecutions, but plaintiffs may still be left without anyone to satisfy judgments in their favour following compensation claims.

Individual Liability

Where an employer is both uninsured and unable to satisfy an award **11–06** of damages, the question arises as to whether individual directors or other officers (assuming that they have the wherewithal to pay damages and are therefore worth suing) may be sued personally by the claimants.

In fact, employers do not always appreciate that any individual, be he director, manager or fellow worker, may be successfully sued if he can be identified as having been negligent or in breach of statutory duty in such a way as to contribute to the injury. The only reason more individuals have not been successfully sued in the past is precisely because compared with employers who are backed by insurance, employers (even directors) are a risky bet in the suing stakes. With increasing uncertainty over the extent of insurance cover, we are likely to see an increasing number of cases where managers, directors, and even fellow workmen are sued as well as or instead of the employer, on the grounds that they are personally liable for the accident or ill-health through some personal failing on their part.

Preservation of Evidence

11–07 A defence to a claim is only as strong as the evidence which can be mustered to support that defence. A plaintiff is usually his own best witness, able to give a first hand account of the circumstances of the accident or of the circumstances in which exposure to, say, noise or respirable dust occurred. By contrast, the defendant is usually struggling to produce cogent first hand accounts of the facts. Allegations may be made of insufficient training, or of a failure to enforce the wearing of personal protective equipment. Three or four years on from an accident (or 30 or 40 years on in the case of some diseases) hard evidence on behalf of the employer is hard to come by. The workplace may have changed out of all recognition, or closed down and been demolished. The workforce may have dispersed; managers and supervisors may have moved away or died.

The next best thing to first hand evidence is a good contemporaneous written record — detailing who attended such and such a training course and on what date; on what date the plaintiff received a set of ear muffs or a pair of goggles. Even better, attendees at training courses, awareness raising videos and recipients of personal protective equipment should sign attendance sheets or receipts. In years to come it may be the only evidence you have that the plaintiff was trained in relation to and protected against the injury of which he now complains. The arrangements necessary to ensure that these records are obtained and are easily retrievable should form part of the health and safety management system.

CHAPTER 12

THE EUROPEAN DIMENSION

Comparing the United Kingdom and the E.C. Approach to Health and Safety

The traditional approach to health and safety in the United Kingdom **12–01** has been empirical and piecemeal. The Common Law, developed over the course of many years, placed general duties upon employers to provide employees with a safe place of work, a safe system of work and safe equipment. It also placed a duty on citizens in general to take reasonable care not to injure their "neighbours" — *i.e.* those persons so closely affected by the acts in question that they ought to have been in the minds of the persons contemplating the acts. The main test for defendants faced with questions of liability was whether they had taken reasonable care so as to avoid injury, and whether the injury was foreseeable. In more recent times many of the common law duties have been supplemented by statutory duties. These are usually more onerous than the duties imposed under common law and some areas are very tightly regulated. Nevertheless, it is often still open to defendants to avoid liability by showing that it was not reasonably practicable to have avoided the breach of duty giving rise to the injury. The underlying approach has been to place fairly general duties upon employers and then to leave it largely up to them to decide how they are going to fulfil them.

The European approach to health and safety on the other hand, and in particular the Directives and Regulations which have emanated from the E.C. have tended to adopt a more coherent approach. They have concentrated on placing detailed and specific duties on employers. The European approach has tended towards the laying down of quantifiable and measurable minimum standards as opposed to the British preference or assessing the reasonableness of particular behaviour or systems.

12–02   The primary engine for bringing about changes in health and safety law within the E.C. is the Directive—formulated and issued by the European Commission which becomes E.C. Law when adopted by the Council of Ministers. Directives do not have direct effect within member states (but see below for important exceptions to this rule) and require domestic legislation within the parliaments of member states to implement them. The European Parliament, whilst it has the right to express an opinion on proposed E.C. policy, has no legislative power.

The Single European Act, which came into force on July 1, 1987, had, as its major objective, the establishment of an internal market by December 31, 1992. However, the Act has also caused a fundamental shift in the balance of power within the E.C. in relation to health and safety. There are two principal reasons for this:

Article 118A—This Article has established a system of majority voting amongst member states in relation to proposed health and safety legislation. It is no longer possible for one state to exercise an effective veto over change and any minority position within the Council of Ministers is correspondingly far weaker.

Article 149—This has strengthened the influence wielded by the European Parliament. In certain areas (including health and safety) it now has an opportunity to express an opinion not only upon the Commission's proposals but also on the position adopted by the Council of Ministers. It therefore now has two opportunities to express a view on each issue. A substantial number of the recommendations made by the Parliament are accepted by both the Commission and the Council of Ministers.

The changes brought about by the Single European Act have raised the profile of health and safety legislation within the E.C. and moved it closer to the centre of the political stage. The European Commission has been galvanised into action and more than 20 health and safety directives as well as numerous other recommendations, covering a wide range of industries and working environments have been adopted in recent years. The increase in the level of activity in the health and safety field can be appreciated when it is considered that during the years between 1970 and 1985 the Council of Ministers adopted no more than six directives specifically designed to improve health and safety at work. The position now is that more than three-quarters of all new health and safety legislation within the United Kingdom originates from the E.C.

The Framework Directive and Its Daughters

The key measure is the Framework Directive for the Introduction of   **12–03** Measures to Encourage Improvements in the Safety and Health of Workers (89/39 1/EEC). This Directive, approved by the Council of Ministers in 1989, was implemented into domestic legislation on the January 1, 1993. Amongst the duties which the Directive places upon employers are duties to evaluate health and safety risks; develop a prevention policy; designate competent personnel; make arrangements for emergency procedures; provide information for workers; allowing workers' representatives time off with pay for appropriate training; and giving workers a right to stop work when faced with imminent danger. Some of the aspects covered in the Framework Directive were already enshrined within United Kingdom law, some were partially covered in the United Kingdom but in less detail than required by the Directive, and some were not covered at all.

A number of "Daughter Directives" made under the authority of the Framework Directive have been adopted. The Daughter Directives which have been formally adopted represent only the tip if the iceberg. A host of detailed and specific directives (some under the authority of the Framework Directive and others independent of it) are at various stages of development and will ensure the complete overhaul of health and safety law within the United Kingdom by the end of the century.

The Effect of European Directives

The traditional rule that E.C. Directives were ineffective in national   **12–04** law until they were implemented into domestic legislation has been steadily eroded since the mid 1980s to the extent that the exceptions to the rule are probably now more important than the rule itself. In

Case 152/84, *Marshall v. Southampton and South West Hampshire Area Health Authority (Teaching)*: [1986] E.C.R. 723; [1986] 1 C.M.L.R. 688, the European Court of Justice held that directives did have direct effect against the Governments of member states. Thus the Area Health Authority, being a direct emanation of the state, was bound by E.C. directives notwithstanding the fact that the United Kingdom Government had not yet implemented the Directive into domestic legislation. Case C–188/89, *Foster v. British Gas*: [1990] I E.C.R. 3313; [1990] 2 C.M.L.R. 833; 1 R.L.R. 353, widened the scope of the *Marshall* decision. The European Court held that the provisions of a Directive could be relied upon against "a body, whatever its legal form, which has been made responsible for providing a public service under the control of the state and has for that purpose special powers beyond those which result from the normal rules applicable in relations between individuals". Nationalised industries, and other companies owned or effectively controlled by the Government, therefore come within the ambit of direct effect.

Case C–106/89, *Marleasing SA v. La Comercial Internacional de Alimentación SA*: [1990] I E.C.R. 4135; [1992] 1 C.M.L.R. 305, has approached the issue from a different direction. In that case the European Court held that domestic Courts, when interpreting E.C. law, must interpret domestic law in the light of existing directives and resolve any conflicts in favour of directives. Thus the position now appears to be that the Framework Directive together with the Daughter Directives which have been adopted are directly binding upon the whole of the public sector in the United Kingdom. Moreover, in any case arising before a British Court (whether involving the public sector or not) where there is a conflict between existing United Kingdom law and a directive then the directive may have supremacy.

Finally, where an individual has lost a right, or a cause of action against an employer because of a failure to implement a European Directive, then it may be that an action will lie against the United Kingdom Government in respect of that failure to implement (Case C–6/90, *Frankovich v. Italian Republic* [1991] I E.C.R. 5357; [1993] 2 C.M.L.R. 66; [1995] I.C.R. 722.

CHAPTER 13

JANUARY 1993

January 1, 1993 is one of the most important dates in the history of **13–01** health and safety law in the United Kingdom. On that day six new far-reaching sets of regulations, together with amendments to some existing legislation, came into force, implementing in part eight E.C. health and safety directives, including the key Framework Directive.

A day to remember and, I thought, quite impossible to write a book of this sort without devoting a chapter to it. In fact, though, I was cautioned against this approach by a very experienced and astute health and safety practitioner. "Don't forget", said the Wise One, "health and safety law wasn't invented in January 1993. If you over-emphasise the "six pack" you'll attach too little importance to all the major legislation which didn't happen to come into force on that date."

In the end I decided to risk it, although I've hedged my bets by devoting the next chapter to other important aspects of safety legislation — both before and after 1993. I still think that the range and depth of the requirements introduced by the six sets of regulations described below sets January 1993 apart from anything which has gone before or since.

The full text of each of the following regulations is set out at Appendices 7 to 12 inclusive.

Management of Health and Safety at Work Regulations 1992

13–02 The key Directive from Europe is the Framework Directive introducing measures to encourage improvements in the safety and health of workers. This Directive was largely implemented into domestic legislation on January 1, 1993 by the Management of Health & Safety at Work Regulations 1992 which create the following duties.

Assessment—Employers must make a suitable and sufficient assessment of the risks to the health and safety of their employees and to non-employees affected by their work. The assessment should identify the measures needed to comply with the relevant statutory provisions. Assessments should be reviewed where it is believed they are no longer valid or where there has been a significant change. Where there are more than five employees, records should be kept of the significant findings and of any group of employees identified as being especially at risk.

Arrangements—Employers must introduce appropriate arrangements for effective planning, organisation, control, monitoring and review of the preventive and protective measures. Where there are five or more employees, the arrangements should be recorded.

Health surveillance—Employers must ensure that their employees are provided with appropriate health surveillance.

Competent persons—Employers must appoint one or more competent persons to assist in undertaking the measures necessary to comply with statutory provisions. A competent person is one who has sufficient training and experience or knowledge and other qualities which enable proper assistance in undertaking such measures.

13–03 **Emergency procedures**—Employers must establish and effect appropriate procedures to be followed in the event of serious and imminent danger and nominate competent persons to implement the evacuation procedures. Workers exposed to such dangers must be informed of the nature of the hazard and the protective steps taken, so far as practicable.

Information—Employers must provide comprehensible and relevant information to employees on risks identified by the assessment, preventive and protective measures, emergency procedures and competent personnel.

Training—In entrusting tasks to employees, employers must take into account their health and safety capabilities. Employers must ensure the provision of health and safety training for employees upon recruitment and on exposure to new or increased risks.

Co-ordination and co-operation—Employers who share a workplace must co-ordinate their respective approaches to health and safety and must co-operate with each other in ensuring compliance. A host employer has particular duties to disclose information to both visiting employers and to the employees of those employers.

Employees' duties—The regulations also impose duties upon individual employees, who are required to use equipment in accordance with instructions, training and statutory requirements. Employees are also under a duty to inform their employers of serious and imminent danger and of shortcomings in the employers' protection arrangements for health and safety.

It can therefore be seen that these regulations provide the central raft for the management of safety in the United Kingdom. Although they are secondary legislation, being regulations made under the Health and Safety at Work etc. Act 1974, in substance they stand on an equal footing with the Act.

The Workplace (Health, Safety and Welfare) Regulations 1992

13–04 The Directive concerning the minimum safety and health requirements for the workplace (commonly known as the Workplace Directive) was introduced via the Workplace (Health, Safety and Welfare) Regulations 1992, and deals with the general facilities and provisions within the workplace. Although wide-ranging, the Workplace Regulations specifically exclude a number of areas, including temporary or mobile work sites (*e.g.* building sites and sites of excavation) and the extractive industries.

The regulations complement the Management of Health and Safety at Work Regulations. If one considers safety at work to be concerned with management of people, and also management of places, then the Management of Health and Safety at Work regulations seek to lay the foundations for the former, while these regulations address the latter.

The requirements of the Workplace Directive relating to fire safety, the provision of information and worker participation are not included in the new Regulations and ACOP. On the other hand, the new Regulations overlap to some extent with the Framework Directive, as Regulation 13(3)(c) is intended to implement Article 6(3)(d) of the Framework Directive (Instructions to be given to workers entering dangerous areas).

The Regulations apply with immediate effect to all new workplaces from January 1, 1993. However "new" relates to use rather than the structure. Workplaces already "in use" before January 1, 1993 had a three-year period of grace and did not have to comply until January 1, 1996, though modification to the structure of an existing workplace would make it new within the meaning of the Regulations.

13–05 A "Workplace" means the place intended to house work stations on the premises of the employer *and* any other place within the area of the undertaking to which the worker has access in the course of his employment. This is a very wide-ranging definition and includes all normal or usual places of work together with any abnormal or unusual places where a worker might be, *provided* that he is properly there on his employer's business.

The extremely wide scope of the Workplace Regulations means that a number of workplaces that were not previously covered by specific statutory requirements will now be subject to the new Regulations. These would include, for example, schools and hospitals.

The Regulations require employers to ensure that every workplace modification extension or conversion under their control complies with any appropriate requirements of the Regulations (see below). A similar duty is placed upon persons who have control over a workplace.

The element of control is an important one, and the Regulations also place duties on persons other than employers to the extent that they control a workplace. This is designed to ensure that there is a clear allocation of responsibility between individual employers and any other person (*e.g.* landlord) who is responsible for services or common facilities.

The Contents of the Regulations

The following requirements are specifically created.   **13–06**

Maintenance—Workplace, equipment, devices and systems must be maintained in an efficient state and working order, and in good repair. Where appropriate, they must be subject to a suitable system of maintenance.

Ventilation—Enclosed workplaces must be ventilated by a sufficient quantity of fresh and purified air.

Temperature—A reasonable temperature must be maintained inside buildings during working hours; a sufficient number of thermometers must be provided.

Lighting—Lighting must be suitable and sufficient, and natural so far as is reasonably practicable. Emergency lighting must be provided where lighting failure would cause danger.

13–07 Cleanliness—Workplaces and furnishings must be kept sufficiently clean. Waste materials, so far as is reasonably practicable, must not accumulate, except in suitable receptacles.

Space—Work rooms must have sufficient floor area, height and unoccupied space. Existing workplaces previously covered by the Factories Act must comply with part 1 of Schedule 1, including a minimum of 11 cubic metres.

Workstations—Must be suitable for the worker and work. A suitable seat must be provided where necessary.

Floors—Must be suitable and not be uneven or slippery, so presenting a safety risk; kept free from obstructions likely to cause a slip, trip or fall, so far as is reasonably practicable. Handrails must be provided on staircases, except where they would obstruct traffic.

13–08 Falls—Suitable and sufficient measures should be taken so far as is reasonably practicable to prevent persons falling or being struck by falling objects. Tanks must be securely covered and fenced where there is risk of a person falling into a dangerous substance.

Windows—Windows and transparent and translucent surfaces must consist of safe material; be clearly marked; and be safe when open.

Traffic—Workplaces must be organised to allow safe circulation by pedestrians and vehicles.

Doors—Doors and gates must be suitably constructed and comply with certain specifications.

Escalators—Must function safely, be equipped with necessary safety devices and be fitted with easily identifiable and readily accessible emergency stop controls.

Sanitation—Suitable and sufficient sanitary conveniences must be **13–09**
provided at readily accessible places. Existing workplaces previously
subject to the Factories Act 1961 must comply with part 11 of
Schedule 1.

Washing—Suitable and sufficient washing facilities must be provided
at readily accessible places.

Water—An adequate supply of wholesome drinking water, and cups,
must be provided, readily accessible and conspicuously marked.

Clothing—Suitable and sufficient accommodation for clothing must
be provided, as well as changing facilities where special clothing is
worn.

Rest—Suitable and sufficient rest facilities must be provided at
readily accessible places. Rest rooms and areas must include suitable
arrangements to protect non-smokers from discomfort. (This, inci-
dentally, is the one and only specific piece of anti-smoking legislation
on the statute book in the United Kingdom). Suitable facilities must
be provided for pregnant or nursing workers to rest; and for workers
to eat meals.

Manual Handling Operations Regulations 1992

Many of the duties under these regulations are not entirely new, but **13–10**
they have never before been so clearly stated in relation to manual
handling tasks.

Manual handling occurs in many work circumstances and is by no
means confined to lifting and carrying. Jobs carrying risks of injuries
may involve the use of tools, pushing materials and components into
place, or supporting components while they are fixed. Many of these
types of jobs are not planned or structured but rather have developed
to meet some need, and as a result the workstations have not been
suitably designed.

More than a quarter of the accidents reported each year to the enforcing authorities are associated with manual handling. The vast majority of reported manual handling accidents result in over three-day injuries, most commonly a sprain or strain, often of the back. Estimates from the United States have suggested that 60 per cent of all money spent on industrial injuries goes to manual handling incidents. The reason is that these types of injuries are very disabling and those injured take a long time to recover, if they recover at all.

13–11   Sprains and strains arise from the incorrect application or prolongation of bodily forces. Poor posture and excessive repetition of movements can be important factors in their onset. Many manual handling injuries are cumulative rather than being attributable to any single handling incident. Sudden or unexpected change of loads, as when the load slips or a large box is lighter than it appears, causes the body muscles to respond disproportionately, and in doing so imposes high loads on the spine.

The Regulations propose an ergonomic approach to identify tasks which are hazardous and to assessing potential solutions. The main requirements are as follows.

Avoid handling—So far as reasonably practicable, avoid the need for employees to undertake any manual handling operations at work which involve a risk of injury.

Assessment—Make a suitable and sufficient assessment, where avoidance is not practicable, of all such operations.

13–12 **Risk reduction**—Take appropriate steps, following assessment, to reduce the risk of injury to the lowest level reasonably practicable.

Information—Take appropriate steps to provide employees undertaking such operations with general indications and, where reasonably practicable, precise information on the weight of each load and the heaviest side of any load whose centre of gravity is not positioned centrally.

Review—Review the assessment where there is reason to suspect that it is no longer valid, or there has been a significant change in the handling operation, and make any changes that are required.

Employees' duties—Employees must make full and proper use of any system of work provided by the employer concerning steps taken to reduce the risk.

Health and Safety (Display Screen Equipment) Regulations 1992

Commonly called the DSE Directive or the VDU (Visual Display Unit) Directive, its full title is the "Directive on Minimum Safety and Health Requirements for Work with Display Screen Equipment". The Directive was implemented on December 31, 1992 by virtue of these regulations.   **13–13**

The main risks associated with DSE work are physical musculoskeletal problems, eye strain and mental stress. The first of these, musculoskeletal problems, is now a well-recognised form of occupational disability, in the form of work related upper limb disorder (WRULD). Two of the most common types of specific diseases are tenosynovitis and carpel tunnel syndrome.

Civil claims for damages from DSE workers alleged to be suffering from one or other form of WRULD are increasingly common. Damages for the physical symptoms can range between £3,000 and £6,000. Where the injury leads to inability to work (and therefore loss of earnings) total damages of up to £60,000 have been recorded.

The following are the main provisions.   **13–14**

Analysis—Suitably and sufficiently analyse workstations used in the undertaking by users and operators, in order to assess risks to health and safety, and to reduce risks to the lowest extent reasonably practicable.

Minimum requirements—Ensure that existing workstations meet minimum requirements contained in a Schedule to the Regulations by December 31, 1996. New workstations coming into existence on or after January 1, 1993 had to comply immediately.

Work routine—Plan the activities of users to ensure that work is interrupted by breaks or changes in activity that reduce their workload at the equipment.

Eyesight—Ensure that users and those about to become users are provided, on request, with an appropriate eye and eyesight test by a competent person. The tests must be provided as soon as practicable for users, and before use for those about to become users; further tests must be provided at regular intervals, and where the user experiences visual difficulties that may reasonably be considered to be caused by DSE work, ensure that users are provided with special corrective appliances for DSE work, where normal corrective appliances are not appropriate.

13–15 Training—Ensure that users, and those about to become users, are provided with adequate health and safety training in the use of the workstation. Training must also be provided following substantial modifications to the workstation.

Information—Ensure the provision of information on measures taken in respect of:

— All aspects of health and safety relating to workstations, and on measures taken in connection with the duties relating to the analysis and minimum requirements for the workstation (to operators and users);

— Daily work routine and training following modifications (to users in the undertaking); and

— Eye and eyesight requirements and initial training (to users employed by the employer).

Personal Protective Equipment at Work Regulations 1992

Commonly referred to as the PPE Health and Safety Directive — the **13–16** full title is the Minimum Health and Safety Requirements for the Use by Workers of Personal Protective Equipment at the Workplace — it is the third of the individual Daughter Directives. It was implemented on January 1, 1993 by these regulations.

There are already a significant number of existing Acts and Regulations which deal with PPE within the United Kingdom. Some of this legislation (particularly the post–Health and Safety at Work Act 1974 legislation) need only be subjected to slight amendments to bring it into line with the Directive. Some of the outdated pre-1974 legislation was repealed by the Regulations (see Schedules 1 and 2 of the Regulations for details).

The important specific duties created by the Regulations are as follows.

Provision—Ensure that suitable PPE is provided to employees who **13–17** may be exposed to risks to their health and safety, except where the risk has been adequately controlled by other means which are equally or more effective.

Suitable—To be "suitable" PPE must be appropriate to the risks and workplace conditions, take account of ergonomic considerations and the state of health of the person wearing the PPE, be capable of fitting the wearer correctly, effective in preventing or adequately controlling the risks involved without increasing the overall risk, so far as is practicable, and comply with any other provision implementing E.C. Directives applicable to PPE.

Compatibility—Ensure that PPE is compatible and effective where it is necessary to use more than one item of PPE.

Assessment—Assess PPE to ensure it is suitable. The assessment must include risks that have not been avoided by other means, the definition of the characteristics needed in the PPE in order to be effective, and comparison between the characteristics of the PPE that is needed and that which is available.

Review—Review the assessment where there is reason to suspect it is no longer valid, or following significant changes, and ensure that any changes required are made.

13–18 Maintenance—Ensure PPE provided to employees is maintained in an efficient state, in efficient working order and in good repair.

Accommodation—Ensure that appropriate accommodation is provided for PPE not in use.

Information—Ensure that the employee is provided with adequate, and appropriate information, instruction and training that is comprehensible.

Use—Take all reasonable steps to ensure that PPE is properly used.

Employees' duties—Use PPE in accordance with training and instruction and return it to the accommodation after use. Employees must also report to the employer any loss or obvious defect in the PPE.

The thrust behind the new Regulations is the identification of hazards and the elimination of the hazard. If elimination is not reasonably practicable, then the hazard has to be reduced to the lowest level possible. Only then should personal protective equipment be used. Personal protective equipment is the last resort, not the first!

Provision and Use of Work Equipment Regulations 1992

The Directive contained general duties relating to safe equipment, **13–19** training, information and consultation. It also contained specific duties relating to minimum requirements for work equipment on particular hazards, such as stability, controls and guarding.

In 1993 certain requirements of the Directive were already covered by existing United Kingdom legislation — in the Health and Safety at Work Act 1974, the Control of Substances Hazardous to Health Regulations 1988, and the Electricity at Work Regulations 1989. However, new Regulations were required to implement those parts of the Directive which were not covered by existing laws and also to repeal existing laws which were outdated or in conflict with the Directive.

The main requirements of the Regulations are as follows.

Suitability—Ensure that work equipment is constructed or adapted **13–20** to be suitable for the purpose for which it is used or provided; have regard to working conditions and risks to health and safety when selecting equipment; and ensure that work equipment is used only for operations for which and under which it is suitable. Suitable means "in any respect which it is reasonably foreseeable will affect the health and safety of any person".

Maintenance—Ensure that work equipment is maintained in an efficient state and working order, and in good repair. Ensure that where there is a maintenance log, it is kept up to date.

Information—Ensure that all persons who use or who supervise the use of work equipment have available to them comprehensible and adequate health and safety information, and where appropriate, written instructions on use. These must also include the conditions and methods of use, and foreseeable abnormal situations and action to be taken in such circumstances.

Training—Ensure all persons who use, or supervise the use of, work equipment have received adequate health and safety training.

Other E.C. requirements—Ensure that work equipment complies with United Kingdom enactments implementing E.C. Directives listed in a Schedule to the Regulations, in respect of work equipment provided for use for the first time after December 31, 1992.

CHAPTER 14

OTHER RELEVANT LEGISLATION

Defective Premises Act 1972

Under section 4 (1) of this Act where a Landlord has an express **14–01** obligation to his Tenant to maintain and repair the premises the Landlord owes to all persons who might reasonably be expected to be affected by defects in the state of the premises a duty to take such care as is reasonable in all the circumstances to see that such persons are reasonably safe from personal injury. This duty extends to an extremely wide category of persons, including visitors, neighbours, passers-by and trespassers. The duty is owned if the Landlord knows, or if he *ought* to have known of the relevant defect.

Under section 4 (4), if the Lease gives the Landlord an express right to enter the premises in order to carry out maintenance or repair work then, as from the date when he is first in a position to exercise the right, he is treated as if he were under an obligation to the Tenant to repair and maintain. However, the Landlord does not owe any duty in respect of any defect in the state of the premises arising from a failure by the Tenant to carry out an obligation expressly imposed upon him.

Under section 6 (2) any duties imposed by this Act are in addition to any other duties (*e.g.* under common law) which a person may owe. Under section 6 (3) any term of an agreement which purports to exclude or restrict the provisions of the Act or any liability arising from it is of no effect.

Occupiers Liability Act 1957

14–02 Under section 2 of the Act an occupier owes a duty to all visitors to take such care as is, in all the circumstances, reasonable to see that the visitor shall be reasonably safe in using the premises for the purposes for which he is invited or permitted by the occupier to be there. The section also provides that in determining whether the occupier has discharged this duty of care regard has to be had to all the circumstances. Sub-section I originally entitled the occupier to extend, restrict, modify or exclude his duty by agreement or otherwise, but this is now over-ridden by section 2 of the Unfair Contract Terms Act 1977, which prohibits an occupier from excluding or restricting by a contract term or notice liability for death or personal injury resulting from negligence where such liability arises in the course of business.

The position of an independent contractor — Under section 2 (4) where damage is caused to a visitor by a danger due to faulty execution of any work of construction, maintenance or repair by an independent contractor employed by the occupier, the occupier is not to be treated as answerable for the danger if in all the circumstances he had acted reasonably in entrusting the work to an independent contractor and had taken such steps as he reasonably ought in order to satisfy himself that the contractor was competent and that the work had been properly done.

Who Is an Occupier?

14–03 The key word here is "control". The test is whether a person has some degree of control associated with and arising from his presence in and use of or activity in the premises. Exclusive occupation is not required and there may be two or more occupiers at any one time. This would certainly extend to a person (or body corporate) who had the immediate power of permitting or prohibiting entry. It would probably also extend to a person or body who controlled or operated common services such as staircases, lifts, and ventilation and heating systems.

Where a Landlord lets the premises to a Tenant, he then is treated as parting with all control, but bear in mind:

— Although a Landlord is not an occupier for the purposes of the Occupiers Liability Act he may still owe certain duties as a Landlord either at common law or under the Defective Premises Act.

— A Landlord is still regarded as the occupier of any parts of the premises retained by him and excluded from the Tenant's holding such as common staircases, lift shafts, entrance hall, etc.

Section 1 of The Occupiers Liability Act 1984 extends the duty of **14–04** care contained in the 1957 Act to trespassers and other persons who have entered premises without the occupier's consent but with lawful authority (*e.g.* in exercise of a private right of way).

Normally a Landlord is not under a duty of care either to his Tenant or to any other person to see that the demised premises are in a safe condition and the common law liability of an occupier has been largely superseded by his statutory duties.

The Electricity at Work Regulations 1989

These regulations impose duties upon employers insofar as they **14–05** relate to matters which are within the employers' control. The word "control" is the key word in these regulations. Where it is clear that either a landlord or a tenant has effective control over an electrical system or particular parts of the system, then it is the landlord or the tenant (as the case may be) who will be regarded as having control over the system, or the relevant parts of it, for the purposes of these regulations.

The central duty of the regulations lies in Regulation 4. This provides that all systems shall be of such construction as to prevent danger; all systems shall be maintained so as to prevent danger; every work activity, including use and maintenance of a system, shall be carried out in such a manner as not to give rise to danger; and any equipment provided for the purpose of protection of persons at work on or near electrical equipment shall be suitable for the use for which it is provided and shall be maintained in a condition suitable for that use. Regulation 5 provides that no electrical equipment shall be put into use where its strength and capability may be exceeded in such a way as to give rise to danger, and Regulation 6 provides that electrical equipment which may be exposed to mechanical damage or to the effects of weather or other environmental hazards shall be of such construction or suitably protected so as to prevent danger from arising. The regulations also lay down provisions in relation to insulation, earthing, isolation, and working on or near live conductors.

The duties under the Electricity at Work Regulations are qualified either by a requirement of reasonable practicability or by a requirement to take reasonable steps and to exercise due diligence.

The Control of Asbestos at Work Regulations 1987

14–06 These regulations are designed to prevent work being undertaken in relation to asbestos unless suitable precautions are taken. Like the COSHH Regulations they apply to employers in relation to both that employer's employees as well as the employees of any other employer who may be affected by the first employer's work activities. In circumstances where COSHH and the Asbestos Regulations would otherwise overlap, the Asbestos Regulations have precedence and the COSHH Regulations do not apply. The key elements of the Asbestos Regulations are:

— Identification of asbestos

— Assessment of risk

— Notification of work with asbestos

— Prevention or reduction of exposure

— Information, training, monitoring and health surveillance

— The setting of action levels and control limits to set maximum exposure levels

14–07 *Identification of Asbestos: Regulation 4*—No work liable to lead to exposure to asbestos is to be commenced unless either the employer has identified the type of asbestos concerned or has in any event taken the maximum recommended safety precautions.

Assessment of Risk: Regulation 5—No work leading to exposure to asbestos is to be carried out unless the employer has made an adequate assessment of that exposure including the steps to be taken to prevent or reduce that exposure to the lowest reasonably practicable level.

Notification of Work with Asbestos: Regulation 6—An employer must not commence work in relation to asbestos unless 28 days' written notice has been provided to the relevant health and safety enforcing authority.

Prevention or Reduction of Exposure: Regulation 8—Every employer **14–08** shall prevent the exposure of employees to asbestos. Where it is not reasonably practicable to prevent such exposure then it must be reduced to the lowest level reasonably practicable by measures other than the use of respirators. Such respirators are only to be used where it is not reasonably practicable to reduce the exposure to below the specified control limits.

Information, Training, Monitoring and Health Surveillance: Regulations 7, 15 and 16—The Asbestos Regulations set out obligations relating to these areas similar to the provisions contained in the COSHH Regulations.

It is important to remember that the Control of Asbestos at Work Regulations apply only to deliberate work with asbestos (*e.g.* stripping asbestos insulation or pipe lagging). Any exposure of persons to "leaking" asbestos other than in the course of deliberate work would be covered by the COSHH Regulations.

The Management of Health and Safety at Work (Amendment) Regulations 1994

These regulations, which came into effect on December 1, 1994, **14–09** implement relevant parts of the E.U.'s Pregnant Worker Directive

(92/85/EEC). The new regulations require employers to assess workplace risks to new or expectant mothers, where there are women of childbearing age within the workforce. The definition in the regulations includes women who have miscarried within the previous six months, as well as women who are pregnant, have given birth or who are breastfeeding. In effect, the regulations will protect such workers for a period of up to six months from having given birth, and for a longer period if breastfeeding continues beyond six months. For practical purposes risk assessments cannot distinguish between women of childbearing age and those who are known to be pregnant.

Where a risk requiring action is identified, but the worker concerned is unable to avoid the risk, her working conditions or hours of work must be changed so as to avoid the risk. If it is not reasonable for the employer to do this then the employer may suspend her, but subject to employment rights protection. Additionally, new or expectant mothers who hold certificates from their G.P.s to the effect that night work is liable to affect their health or safety may also be suspended from work, with protection of employment rights.

Control of Substances Hazardous to Health Regulations 1994

14–10 These regulations, which came into force recently, incorporate as a single legislative package all three previous COSHH Regulations. The new regulations implement the Biological Agents Directive (90/679/EEC) and extend the regulations to the offshore oil and gas industry. The regulations also set new or revised maximum exposure limits for nine substance groups and involve small changes affecting short term maximum exposure limits.

The COSHH Regulations place duties upon employers both in relation to their own employees and also to persons employed by other employers who may be affected by the first employer's activities. The duties extend to the following areas:

— Assessment of risks

— Prevention or control of exposure

— Monitoring

— Health surveillance

— Information and training

Assessment of Risk—An employer shall not carry on any work which **14–11** is liable to expose any employees to any substance hazardous to health unless there has first been made a suitable and sufficient assessment of the risks created by that work and the steps that need to be taken in order to control those risks. The assessment needs to be reviewed whenever there is reason to suspect that it is no longer valid or where there has been a significant change in the work to which the assessment relates.

Prevention or Control of Exposure—A duty is placed upon employers to ensure that exposure to substances hazardous to health is either prevented or, where this is not reasonably practicable, adequately controlled. Wherever reasonably practicable, such prevention or control is to be achieved by measures other than the provision of personal protective equipment.

Monitoring Exposure—Where it is necessary to adequately control the exposure of employees to substances hazardous to health or where it is otherwise necessary to protect the health of employees, the employer shall ensure that exposure of employees to substances hazardous to health is monitored. Where particular substances are the subject of exposure limits, COSHH lays down the specific frequency of monitoring operations.

Health Surveillance—Employees who are identified as being at risk **14–12** from substances hazardous to health should be placed under regular health surveillance, where there are valid techniques for detecting indications of the effect of the exposure.

Information and Training—Any employer who undertakes work which may expose employees to substances hazardous to health shall provide those employees with suitable and sufficient information confirming the risks to health created by the exposure as well as the precautions which should be taken. This information should include the results of any monitoring. Employees should also be informed forthwith if the results of monitoring show that maximum exposure limits have been exceeded.

COSHH also prohibits the use of certain substances at work and sets exposure limits with regard to certain other substances.

Construction (Design and Management) Regulations 1994

14–13 The Regulations come into force on March 31, 1995, although there was a nine-month transition period for projects already in progress. They implement most of the 1992 Temporary or Mobile Worksites Directive.

The Regulations place duties on five key "parties" and introduce the important concepts of a health and safety plan and file. They do not cover construction work which:

— Is not notifiable (*i.e.* it lasts less than 30 days and involves 500 person days or less); and

— Involves four or less people.

A breach of duty under the Regulations does not confer a right of action in any civil proceedings. The only exceptions are the duties on the client to ensure that the construction phase does not start before the safety plan has been prepared, and on the principal contractor to ensure that only authorised personnel are allowed on-site during construction.

The Main Duties

14–14 The client must be satisfied that each of the four categories below are competent and ensure the allocation of sufficient resources, including time, to the project; and ensure that work does not begin until a satisfactory health and safety plan has been prepared.

The **designer** must ensure that structures are designed to avoid and minimise risks during construction and maintenance; provide adequate information where risks cannot be avoided; and alert clients to their duties.

The **planning supervisor** has overall responsibility for coordinating the health and safety aspects of the design and planning phase. The supervisor is responsible for the early stages of the health and safety plan, and must ensure that the health and safety file is prepared and delivered to the client at the end of the project.

The **principal contractor** must develop and implement the plan; **14–15** take account of safety issues when preparing and presenting tenders; coordinate the activities of contractors to ensure compliance with safety legislation; check on the provision of information and training for employees, and on consultation arrangements with employees and the self-employed; and ensure only authorised personnel are allowed on-site.

Contractors must cooperate with the principal contractor and provide relevant information on the risks to safety arising from their work and on the means of control, and provide information to the principal contractor and to employees. The self-employed have similar duties to contractors.

The health and safety plan covers two phases. At pre-tender stage, it must include a general description of the work, timings, details of risks to workers, and information for the principal contractors and on welfare arrangements. At construction stage, it must include arrangements for the health and safety of all those affected by the construction work, arrangements for the management of the work and for monitoring of legal compliance, and information about welfare arrangements.

The health and safety file contains information for the client or user of the building on the risks present during maintenance, repair or renovation.

CHAPTER 15

ENFORCEMENT AND THE ENFORCERS

Workplace health and safety legislation and standards are enforced, **15–01** depending upon the nature of the workplace, either by the Health and Safety Executive or by the Environmental Health Departments of local authorities. The former is the executive arm of the Health and Safety Commission, which formulates policy and advises government. Both the HSE and the HSC were created by the Health and Safety at Work etc. Act 1974. The powers of the HSE (and also EHOs) are derived from that Act, although many of the functions carried out by the HSE were formerly performed by a number of separate inspectorates.

Broadly, the HSE enforces in industrial workplaces, including most construction sites, factories, mines, quarries, railways and off-shore installations; local authorities enforce in retail outlets and offices (see Appendix 5 for a definitive list).

Powers of Enforcers

I am often puzzled by the attitude which some owners of businesses, **15–02** directors, and senior managers display towards inspectors. They don't take these people seriously enough. Some do. Some are *very* smart in the way they handle those who enforce legislation. But most are not — and in the end they are the losers. Most professional safety managers, or quality directors, are aware of the need to establish a good working relationship with inspectors, but often they have too many internal battles of their own to fight to really succeed in getting the message across to line managers.

I frequently ask clients who they think (professionally speaking) is the most important person in their lives outside their own organisation. After they have exhausted every conceivable stakeholder I surprise them with the knowledge that their local inspector is that very person! He is probably (unless they are wholly dependent on one customer or supplier) the only person who has the power to close them completely, at no notice and without a court order.

15–03 Health and Safety Executive Inspectors and Environmental Health Officers enjoy the following powers:

— To enter premises at any reasonable time, or at *any* time where in his opinion there is a dangerous situation

— To inspect and to take copies of records

— To require signed statements from persons able to provide relevant information

— To take measurements, photographs and recordings

— To take samples

— To direct that premises remain undisturbed

15–04 Among the more important powers available to Inspectors are a right of entry on to premises in order to carry out their duties and a right to obtain written statements from those persons whom Inspectors reasonably believe to be able to help them in their investigations. It should be noted that a statement made by a person pursuant to this statutory power cannot be used as evidence against the maker of that statement — although it can be used as evidence against other persons, or the employer of the person who has made the statement. Further, evidence sufficient to prosecute a person who has made a statement may be obtained from other sources (including statements made by other persons). As Inspectors enjoy a statutory right to compel persons to make statements it is not strictly necessary for them to invite witnesses to make statements under caution (*i.e.* under the conditions imposed by the Police and the Criminal Evidence

Act). Statements made voluntarily, under caution, **may be** used in evidence against the makers of the statements.

Employers may come into contact with inspectors either as a result of accidents or other occurrences which have been reported, or during the course of routine inspections. Prosecutions and enforcement notices may result from either type of contact but, on the whole, are more likely to arise as a result of reported accidents than compliance issues emerging during routine inspections. Inspectors adopt a hierarchy of responses to offences, depending upon the seriousness of the offence or offences. The starting point is a formal warning to the employer, followed by the issue of an enforcement notice. Prosecutions are generally reserved for offences which cannot be adequately dealt with by either of the above two means.

Obstruction

It is an offence to intentionally obstruct an Inspector or to knowingly or recklessly make a false statement. Obstruction is punishable by a maximum fine of £5,000, and is triable in the Magistrates' Court only.   **15–05**

Approved Codes of Practice

These are issued under Section 16 of HSWA 1974 and include guidance on compliance with statutory requirements. Breach of ACOP does not automatically amount to an offence, *but* the fact of a breach can be used as evidence to prove that an offence has been committed. The Defendant has to show that the precautions which he took were equally as effective as compliance with the ACOP.   **15–06**

Dealing with the Inspectorate

Needless to say, the ideal relationship with the Inspectorate is one of openness in which employers can take advantage of advice and   **15–07** information available from inspectors without the risk of constantly laying themselves open to criticism and a zealous attention to nit-picking detail. Although the attitude of some individual inspectors and managers would make it quite impossible for relationships to enter this happy state, in general, employers have more to gain than to lose by showing a co-operative and positive attitude toward the Inspectorate. When changes in systems of work or the introduction of new technology have implications for health and safety, it is often worthwhile seeking the views of the Inspectorate. This is never more true than when employers are considering deviating from the terms of an approved code of practice. Whilst the approval of the inspectorate is not a legal requirement of such deviation, it is a clear advantage for an employer. Of course, such approval renders a prosecution based on failure to comply with an ACOP extremely unlikely. Just as important, where the Inspectorate refuses to commit itself it renders any future proceedings based upon failure difficult, in view of the opportunity given to the Inspectorate to comment and advise.

Enforcement Policy

15–08   Under a degree of political pressure to present a "user-friendly" face to employers, the HSC and HSE have published a number of documents which seek to explain its policies and the criteria upon which it bases its decisions. These include "Working with Employers", "Your Rights when Health and Safety Inspectors Take Action", and "Enforcement Policy Statement". Although these do not formally bind Local Authority Environmental Health Departments, a liaison committee consisting of representatives of HSE and EHOs tries to ensure consistency of approach.

The "Enforcement Policy Statement" sets out four principles of enforcement: proportionality; consistency; transparency; and targeting.

15–09   *Proportionality*—Under this principle enforcement action should be in proportion to any risk to health and safety and the seriousness of breaches of legislation. Where significant risks exist then the duty holder (usually the employer or the occupier) must take preventive measures unless the cost is clearly excessive compared with the benefits.

Consistency—Similar actions should be taken in similar circumstances in order to achieve similar outcomes. In particular arrangements should exist to promote the consistent exercise of discretion.

Transparency—Inspectors must distinguish between statutory requirements on the one hand and advice or guidance on the other. Employers should be helped to understand what is expected of them and what they can expert from inspectors.

Targeting—Resources should be concentrated on those activities which give rise to the most serious dangers or where the hazards are not well controlled. Enforcement action should be concentrated upon those who are best placed to control the risk.

In "Working with Employers" (which is a "Citizens Charter" **15–10** document) the HSE explain their performance criteria. They commit themselves to being courteous; to being fair and consistent; and to identifying themselves on all occasions when dealing with employers or members of the public. They aim to reply to all enquiries or complaints within 10 working days. Normally, where the HSE write to an employer following a visit they will do so within 15 working days. Apparently the response time target is met in over 90 per cent of cases.

Clearly the HSE are making an effort to establish a more productive relationship with employers generally. Although this philosophy may not have worked its way down to some individual inspectors, by and large there has not been a better time for employers to achieve better working arrangements with inspectors in a way that, in the long run, can only be of benefit to those employers.

CHAPTER 16

ENFORCEMENT NOTICES

What Are They?

Health and safety enforcement notices are of two kinds: improve- **16-01** ment notices and prohibition notices. The enforcement agencies have the power to serve these notices and individual inspectors may be authorised to issue them. Both types of enforcement notice could be served either because of a routine visit by an inspector or, more commonly, because of a specific incident or accident at premises (although the HSE is stepping up its programme of routine visits particularly to small and medium sized companies).

Depending on the severity of the problem which an inspector finds at the site, the procedure may be that a formal warning is issued before an enforcement notice. The guidance on employers' rights referred to in Chapter 15 enables employers to make informal representations before an improvement notice is served. Whenever an inspector intends to issue such a notice an employer has a right to a written explanation of what is wrong, an outline of what is required to be done and by when. The employer then has two weeks to make representations to the inspector's manager before a notice can be served.

Why Are Enforcement Notices Served?

Improvement Notices

16–02 An improvement notice may be served where an inspector believes that an employer is contravening statutory provisions, or has contravened such provisions and the circumstances are such that this contravention will continue or be repeated.

The Notice served will state that the inspector is of the opinion that either of the above conditions exists, and will specify which statutory provision the inspector believes is being breached. The notice will also give reasons as to why the inspector holds that opinion, and will give a period in which the breach is to be rectified. In any event, the time limit given for complying with the notice must not be less than 21 days.

Notices can be served on companies as well as individuals.

Failure to comply with any aspect of an improvement notice is a criminal offence. This is particularly important where the notice has been served on an individual (for example, the company director).

Prohibition Notices

16–03 There are two significant points to note on prohibition notices. The first is that, in extreme cases, a prohibition notice can be drafted so that it effectively shuts down the entirety of an employer's business, until the situation highlighted by the inspector in the notice has been remedied. The second point is that when serving a valid prohibition notice, there is no need for an inspector to prove that there has been any breach of statutory provisions — all that is necessary is a situation where there is a risk of serious injury. Furthermore, a notice may be drafted so as to take effect immediately.

An inspector may serve a prohibition notice if activities at the site are carried on or are likely to be carried on in such a way that there is a risk of serious personal injury. The risk of injury need not necessarily be to an employee of the company.

A prohibition notice will state that the inspector believes there is a risk of serious personal injury and will specify the matters which, in the inspector's opinion, give or will give rise to the risk. It will also specify which statutory provisions, if any, are being breached. It will further direct that the activities that are the subject of the notice must not be carried on by or under the control of the person or company on whom the notice is served, until the defect highlighted by the inspector has been rectified.

As with improvement notices, a prohibition notice may be served either on a company or an individual.

Further Provisions Regarding Improvement/Prohibition Notices

Improvement and prohibition notices may include directions as to **16–04** remedial measures which the person or company served may take to comply. The directions may refer to any of the approved codes of practice, and may be drafted so as to offer the person or company served with a choice of methods of remedying the problem.

Inspectors may not use improvement notices to require remedial measures to a building which are more onerous than are currently required by the building regulations. The only exception to this is where the statutory provision which the inspector is claiming has been breached imposes a higher standard than is found in the building regulations.

Neither an improvement notice nor a prohibition notice may be served in respect of fire escapes unless consultation has first taken place with the fire authority.

With the exception of a prohibition notice which has immediate **16–05** effect, any other prohibition or improvement notice may be withdrawn before the end of the period which the notice gives for defects to be remediated. Likewise, the period for compliance specified in a notice may be extended at any time by an inspector, unless the person or company served with the notice is appealing against it.

Finally, following the passing of the Environment Act in 1995 the HSE no longer has power to serve improvement or prohibition notices in respect of emissions into the atmosphere. Such notices can now only be served by the Environment Agency (or the Scottish Environmental Protection Agency where appropriate).

Appeals

16–06 A person or company on whom an improvement or prohibition notice has been served may appeal against a notice to an industrial tribunal. The appeal should be made within 21 days from the date of service of the notice (although the tribunal has discretion to extend that time period).

In the case of an improvement notice, the bringing of an appeal has the effect of suspending the operation of the notice until the appeal is heard by the tribunal (unless the appeal is first withdrawn). For prohibition notices, the fact that an appeal has been brought will not suspend the operation of the notice *unless* the industrial tribunal so directs. Even if such a direction is given, the notice is only suspended from the date of that direction.

On appeal, it is for an inspector to prove that the statutory requirements for service of an enforcement notice have been made out in the particular case before the tribunal. Thereafter, it is for the appellant to show good reason why the notice could not be complied with. Both the inspector and the appellant are required to prove their evidence to the civil standard of a balance of probabilities.

The industrial tribunal will then either cancel the notice, affirm it, or affirm it subject to modifications.

Offences

16–07 It is a criminal offence to fail to comply with an improvement or prohibition notice (including any such notice as modified on appeal). On summary conviction (*i.e.* in the Magistrates' Court) the penalty is imprisonment for a term not exceeding six months, or a fine not exceeding £20,000, or both. In the Crown Court (*i.e.* on indictment), the sanction is possible imprisonment for a term not exceeding two years, or an unlimited fine, or both.

Legislative Source

16–08 Section 21 of the Health and Safety at Work Act etc. 1974 governs the service by inspectors of improvement notices.

Section 22 deals with prohibition notices, and section 23 contains supplementary provisions on enforcement notices. Section 24 governs the appeals procedure.

CHAPTER 17

PROSECUTION

A criminal prosecution sits at the top of the hierarchy of the range of **17–01**
responses open to the enforcement agencies. It is the ultimate
sanction, signifying that the enforcer takes a serious view of the
alleged offences, and that an enforcement notice (and even more so
a warning) would not be an adequate response. This is not to say that
prosecutions and enforcement notices are mutually exclusive, and I
have come across cases where both an improvement notice and a
prosecution have arisen out of the same set of facts.

In purely economic terms, of course, it is possible that in some
circumstances a prohibition notice may have a more serious effect on
business performance than criminal proceedings. As pointed out in
Chapter 16, it is perfectly possible for a prohibition notice to bring
the production process, or a key part of it, to a complete standstill —
in extreme cases cutting off revenue. In only the gravest prosecutions, accompanied by the most savage fines, will the direct financial
cost of criminal proceedings amount to more than a small percentage
of annual turnover.

However, perhaps unsurprisingly, most employers seem to share **17–02**
the view that a prosecution is the most unwelcome intervention
which the law can make. Financial considerations are usually secondary. Uppermost in employers' minds are the attendant publicity;
fears over loss of business (particularly if the employer is a contractor
who depends upon a good safety record to strengthen tenders); a
profound sense of management failure; and the sheer disagreeable-
ness of acquiring a criminal record. These broader concerns emerged
in a recent case where a major international drinks company pleaded
guilty to two offences. In his speech in mitigation the defendant's
lawyer told the court that whatever financial penalty the court might

impose would be as nothing compared to the loss of face and reputation which the defendant had already suffered. This comment, though admirably frank, might have rather underplayed the financial consequences of a conviction. At any rate the court, perhaps rising to a challenge, promptly imposed the maximum fine on both counts!

Dealing with a prosecution involves an employer in a number of sometimes difficult exercises and decisions: gathering and evaluating evidence; choosing whether to plead guilty or not guilty; and, in many cases, deciding whether to opt for a crown court trial in front of a jury. This process should begin even before the summons initiating the proceedings is served.

Stage 1 — Pre-Summons

17–03 The best way to defend a health and safety prosecution is not to get one in the first place. The period of time (which may be several months) which elapses between the relevant incident or inspection and the arrival of a summons is therefore an important stage, which too few employers seek to use to their advantage.

When the HSE inspector or environmental health officer has completed his investigation there then ensues a decision-making process within the agency concerned. The inspector will make a recommendation — whether to prosecute and, if so, on which charges. The recommendation and the inspector's report and statements will be considered by senior officers before any final decision is taken. The Enforcement Policy Statement referred to in Chapter 15 clarifies the circumstances in which prosecution will be considered. It states that proceedings will be taken where

> "it is appropriate in the circumstances as a way to draw general attention to the need for compliance with the law and the maintenance of standards required by law, especially where there would be a normal expectation that a prosecution would be taken or where, through the conviction of offenders, others may be deterred from similar failures to comply with the law. Or where there is judged to have been potential for considerable harm arising from the breach. Or where the gravity of the offence taken with the general record and approach of the offender warrants it."

As regards proceedings against individuals the Statement makes it clear that enforcement agencies will "identify and prosecute ... individuals including company directors and managers if they consider a conviction is warranted and can be secured."

Obviously there will be some cases where, as a result of the particular facts, a prosecution is inevitable, whatever the employer does following the incident. In many other cases the employers' influence over the decision-making process will be non-existent. However, at the margins there will be some finely balanced cases where the employers' actions and attitude *after* the incident will have a material bearing on the decision on whether to proceed with a prosecution. In particular if there are evidential points which are favourable to the employer then it is very much in his interests to make sure that they are brought to the attention of the inspector and reflected in his report. Now, most inspectors would take the view that their investigations are even-handed and that any points favourable to the employer are taken fully into account. Unfortunately, although this is usually the case it is not always so. Because inspectors are human standards of investigation vary. Employers who take an entirely passive attitude to investigations run the risk that the inspector will miss points which are in their favour. Generally, anything which is to the employers' credit should emerge at the investigation stage, rather than be left to the trial. A prosecution averted is preferable to one successfully defended.

17–04

Stage 2 — Pre-Trial

The stage following service of the summons but prior to the trial is one in which crucial decisions are made. How to plead? Guilty or not guilty? This decision will largely be informed by the evidence. Both the evidence obtained by the inspector upon which the prosecution rely (the defendant is entitled to see this or to have it presented to him in summary form) and any evidence gathered by his own lawyers and expert witnesses.

17–05

Although the weight of evidence will determine the plea in most cases, other factors can also play a part. In some cases commercial considerations are paramount. Where a conviction would substantially reduce an employer's chances of successful tenders he may be more inclined to plead not guilty, even though the weight of evidence is against him. Commercial factors can also work in the opposite direction. I recall a case where both supplier and customer were prosecuted as a result of the same incident. The only possibility of a successful defence for either defendant lay in a "cutthroat defence" — *i.e.* seeking to blame the other defendant. Rather than take this route the supplier preferred to enter a guilty plea. The supplier was over-reliant on the customer, and his prime concern was the maintenance of his commercial relationship. He thought (probably rightly) that this relationship would be put at risk by the allegations which he would be required to level against his customer in order to establish his own innocence.

17–06 Another important decision which has to be taken at this stage is the mode of trial. Under English law serious offences are said to be "indictable" and are tried in Crown Court, under a judge and in front of a jury. Lesser offences are dealt with in the Magistrates' Court by way of "summary" trial. Most breaches of safety legislation do not fall automatically into one or other category, but are triable "either way". These cases are initiated in the Magistrates' Court and the defendant can choose, if he wishes, to elect trial in the Crown Court instead. If the defendant is content for the case to remain in the Magistrates' Court then the Magistrates must decide whether to keep it. If they consider the offence to be sufficiently serious they can themselves remit it to the Crown Court for trial. In reaching their decision they will take into account views expressed on behalf of both the prosecution and the defence.

It is unusual for defendants to elect a jury trial in the Crown Court. The consequences of a conviction are greater — reflecting the seriousness of the charge. Offences which carry a maximum fine of £5,000 or £20,000 in the Magistrates' Court are unlimited in the Crown Court. Those offences which carry a prison sentence are similarly differentiated — with a maximum term of six months in the Magistrates' Court but two years in the Crown Court. The legal costs of defending the proceedings will inevitably be greater in the Crown Court and the proceedings longer, and likely to generate more publicity.

Stage 3 — Trial

Where a defendant enters a guilty plea the trial itself is relatively **17–07** short — often occupying no more than a half day of court time. The prosecution will outline the facts and emphasise any points which it considers to be especially important. The defendant's representative will make a statement in mitigation, drawing attention to factors which the defendant wishes the court to take into account when deciding sentence. These might, for example, include a previously good record, the defendant's response to the incident giving rise to the case, or the prompt entry of a guilty plea. The most effective mitigation statements are those which are short and to the point. Other than for the most compelling reasons attempts to shift the blame to other parties (particularly employers who are not defendants in the case, or the injured workman himself) are best avoided as being counter-productive.

A contested trial — following the entry of a plea of not guilty — is a far more complex, costly and time-consuming event. It may easily engage court time of a week or so, or several weeks in some cases. The effort and time needed to prepare for the trial is correspondingly enlarged. For most employers, especially small and medium sized enterprises, the time factor is a discouragement to a contested trial. Before committing themselves to a not guilty plea I like employers to be fully aware of what demands that decision is going to place upon the organisation. "Never mind the rights and wrongs of the proceedings, or the strength of the evidence — can you afford the time and disruption of a full trial?"

Final Thoughts

The HSE's success rate in its prosecutions is impressive, in recent **17–08** years between eight and nine out of every ten prosecutions has consistently ended in a conviction. These figures are not entirely a tribute to the HSE's trial skills. I believe that this high success rate reflects a very conservative policy towards criminal proceedings. I frequently tell managers who think that their organisations are put upon by enforcement agencies that far more prosecutions could be brought than in fact are pursued. After all, only a tiny fraction of accidents which give rise to successful civil claims for damages result in prosecution. Whilst not every such accident would necessarily also result in a conviction (because of, amongst other things, differences in the standard of proof) clearly a good many would. The truth is that many accidents or circumstances which would almost certainly, if pursued, result in a conviction are not proceeded with. This may be because the enforcement agency does not consider it appropriate to prosecute in the particular circumstances, or simply because the incident does not come to the agency's attention at all (which, if it is not a reportable accident, disease or occurrence, it is not likely to).

CHAPTER 18

FATAL ACCIDENTS

Workplace accidents which result in a fatality, or fatalities, give rise   **18–01**
to special considerations. All of the enforcement machinery
described in the preceding three chapters is equally as relevant to
fatal accidents as it is to any other example of workplace injury or ill-
health. In addition, however, a number of other legal factors come
into play. The first of these which deserves consideration (as it will
arise in relation to every work-related death) is the Coroner's
Inquest.

Inquests

A Coroner's Inquest is one of the oldest courts to exercise jurisdic-   **18–02**
tion under English law. It has survived, remarkably intact, since
medieval times. It can be distinguished from most other forms of
legal proceedings in that it is an *inquisitorial* procedure. It is a fact-
finding forum. It does not adjudicate between competing parties.
    The main purpose of the inquest is to establish the facts relevant to
the death. What was the identity of the deceased? When and where
did death occur? What was the medical cause of death and how did
the deceased die? In most workplace-related inquests it is usually
only the last of these questions which is likely to excite any con-
troversy, as it calls for a verdict to be delivered. One possible verdict,
that the deceased was unlawfully killed, implies that death resulted
from the commission of a criminal offence.

18–03 In all workplace-related deaths the Coroner will sit with a jury and it is the jury, under the guidance of the Coroner, who will frame the verdict, having listened to the evidence. The deceased's estate and dependents are entitled to be represented at the inquest, as is the enforcement agency to which the accident was reported and which investigated it. Anyone else with a proper interest in the outcome of the proceedings may also be represented, including the deceased's employer and that employer's insurers. The range of verdicts open to the jury is hardly a testament to the clarity of the law. Overwhelmingly the most common verdict in workplace-related inquests are "accidental death" or "death by misadventure". Legally, there is no difference between those two verdicts and the Court of Appeal has, on separate occasions, attempted to discourage the use of the "misadventure" verdict in favour of the rather more straightforward "accidental death". Some Coroners, however, still persist in directing juries in relation to both verdicts, presenting them as alternatives — often to the visible confusion of members of the jury.

Put simply, both verdicts mean that, in the jury's view, the deceased died other than from natural causes in circumstances which did not result from either murder, manslaughter or suicide. "Accidental death" is something of a misnomer and does not imply that the death was accidental in the sense that it did not result from negligent acts (either of the deceased himself or other) or breach of statutory duty by the employer. The verdict is not therefore at all incompatible with a successful damages claim against the employer by the deceased's family.

18–04 A verdict of "unlawful killing" can only mean that, in the view of the jury, the death resulted from an act of either murder or manslaughter. Of course, in the vast majority of such cases no one seriously thinks that a murder has been committed. The practical implication of the verdict therefore is that the jury considers someone, or some organisation, to be guilty of manslaughter. No inquest verdict can be framed in such a way as to indicate that named individuals or organisations are either criminally or civilly liable in respect of the death. In some cases it is, in practice, quite obvious who the verdict is aimed at. In other cases however it is quite impossible to tell who the jury considers to be responsible for the unlawful killing. This is particularly so where the deceased was employed by contractors and was killed on a multi-employer work site (such as a construction site or an offshore platform).

The inability of a jury to be more specific, in its verdict, as to where responsibility for the death lies may be thought unnecessarily restrictive. It does however need to be set in the context of the inquisitorial nature of an inquest and the sometimes haphazard way in which evidence is presented. As there are no competing parties at an inquest there are no formal allegations. An employer does not therefore, as he would in a civil or criminal court, have an opportunity to consider specific allegations and deal with them in the way he thinks fit. Neither does he have an opportunity to call evidence himself, on his own behalf, as it is the Coroner who calls the evidence. The restriction on naming individuals or organisations is one of the necessary checks and balances built into the system. It helps to prevent unfair allegations of manslaughter being seen to be levelled at particular individuals or bodies on the basis of inadequate or incomplete evidence.

An inquest verdict is not conclusive so far as other legal proceedings are concerned and has no direct effect on the outcome of those proceedings. Of course, in practical terms, the evidence which is given at an inquest may assist either party in any subsequent criminal or civil proceedings. An "unlawful killing" verdict will prompt consideration, or reconsideration, of manslaughter charges by the Police and Crown Prosecution Service. But it does not necessarily follow that such charges will follow the verdict.

Manslaughter

The HSE's Enforcement Policy Statement referred to in Chapter 15 **18–05** states that where there has been a breach of the law leading to a work related death, then enforcing authorities need to consider whether the circumstances of the case might justify the charge of manslaughter.

The crime of manslaughter is a common law offence and, in the context of senior managers and directors, involves liability through a breach of duty of care arising from gross negligence. The ingredients of the offence were examined in the case *R. v. Prentice and Others* (1993 4 All E.R. 935 C.A.). In that case the Court held that gross negligence sufficient to secure a manslaughter conviction could arise in one of four circumstances:

1. Where the Defendant had failed to appreciate a clear and obvious risk

2. Where the Defendant having appreciated that a clear and obvious risk existed, nevertheless decided to run that risk

3. Where there was appreciation of the risk coupled with a wholly inadequate attempt to avoid it

4. Where there was inattention or failure on the part of the Defendant to advert to a serious risk going beyond mere inadvertence

18–06 Prosecutions for manslaughter against directors arising from work or other safety related fatalities have increased in recent years. Several directors of P&O European Ferries were prosecuted following the capsize of the Herald of Free Enterprise in March 1987. Those prosecutions failed on the basis that there was insufficient evidence to convict any of the named individuals. In 1989, in the case of *R. v. Holt* (*Health and Safety Information Bulletin* 169, January 1990), the first United Kingdom conviction of a company director following a workplace accident was secured. Norman Holt pleaded guilty to manslaughter and was sentenced to 12 months imprisonment suspended for two years. The Judge in that case said that he was imposing a lenient sentence on Holt, as this was the first case of its type, but that subsequent Defendants could not expect to be dealt with so leniently. In 1994, in *R. v. Kyte* (*Health and Safety Bulletin* 229, January 1995), the first immediate custodial sentence was imposed upon a company director following a manslaughter conviction. Peter Kyte was the Managing Director of Oll, the leisure company which owned and operated the activity centre at Lyme Bay where four teenagers drowned in a canoeing accident in March 1993. Mr Kyte was sentenced to three years imprisonment (later reduced to two years on appeal). It is interesting to note that Mr Kyte's main place of work was not at the activity centre itself, and that the manager of the centre, employed by Oll, was acquitted of manslaughter.

It should also be noted that the companies of which Norman Holt and Peter Kyte were directors were both relatively small companies with very simple management structures, in which directors took an active part in a range of operational managerial activities. In practice the position seems to be, rightly or wrongly, that it is easier to secure a conviction against a director of a small company with a simple management structure than against a director of a large company involved in multifarious activities with a complex management structure. This is because in the latter case (where responsibilities tend to be divided up) it is more difficult to identify individual directors who have both the requisite knowledge of specific risks and the responsibility and authority to avert them.

The Lyme Bay canoeing tragedy also resulted in the company, Oll, **18–07** being convicted of manslaughter. This was the first occasion in the United Kingdom upon which a corporate body had been found guilty of that crime. There had previously been three unsuccessful attempts to prosecute corporate bodies for manslaughter, the most recent against P&O European Ferries Limited, arising out of the capsize of the Herald of Free Enterprise. That case established that it was possible, in principle, for a corporate body to be guilty of manslaughter, subject to the evidence in the individual case. In *R. v. Oll* (*Health and Safety Bulletin* 229, January 1995) the company was found guilty of manslaughter on the basis that the managing director represented the "governing mind" of the company itself. As the law stands at the moment, it is not possible to add together, in a cumulative fashion, individual failings on the part of other members of management or other employees with a view to establishing a manslaughter conviction against a corporate body on the basis of aggregate fault. The Law Commission has recommended the introduction of a new statutory crime of manslaughter which would enable corporate bodies to be convicted independently of the guilt of individual directors or managers. It remains to be seen whether such an offence will find its way onto the statute book in the near future.

APPENDIX 1

OUTLINE SAFETY POLICY

Blank Company
Health and Safety Policy

1. Introduction

1.1　This is the general Health and Safety Policy ("the Policy") of **A1–01**
BLANK I ("the Company"). It applies to all directors, managers and other employees ("the employees") of the Company and has been prepared for their benefit in accordance with the Health & Safety at Work Act 1974 and other relevant statutory provisions.

1.2　A number of statements supplemental to the Policy have been and will continue to be made by the Company dealing with specific Health and Safety Policy areas.

1.3　The Policy reflects the Company's recognition that the implementation of safe working practices and accident prevention are an important responsibility of management and essential to the successful management of the Company.

2. The Policy

A1–02 2.1   It is the policy of the Company that, so far as is reasonably practicable, effective steps will be taken to ensure the health and safety of:

2.1.1   All its employees whilst at work;

2.1.2   Any other person or persons affected by the undertaking of the Company;

2.1.3   Any lawful visitors to Company premises.

2.2   The Company regards health and safety as a management responsibility of primary importance. All levels of management shall give a high priority to their duties relating to health and safety over other duties that they may have.

A1–03 2.3   The Company recognises that it has a responsibility to create and maintain safe systems of work and a safe working environment. The Company will take all steps as are reasonably practicable and within its authority and control to meet that responsibility and implement this Policy. The requirements of the Health and Safety at Work Act 1974 and all legislation relevant to it shall be regarded as the standard of health and safety to be implemented and practised by the Company.

2.4   The Company will continue to make available resources (including finance and expertise) to provide working conditions that are as healthy and safe as reasonably practicable.

2.5   The Company will ensure that its employees are provided with appropriate information, instruction, training and supervision to enable them safety to carry out their duties in a safe working environment.

A1–04 2.6   The Company will place a high priority on health and safety in specifying and purchasing materials, equipment and substances for use in its premises.

2.7   Upon the introduction of new working practices and technology the Company will continue to ensure, so far as reasonably practicable, that those working practices and procedures and equipment are safe and that appropriate training is given.

2.8   The Company will continue to arrange for specific policy statements to be issued and annexed to this Policy as required to secure the health and safety of those to whom the Policy applies.

2.9   The Company welcomes suggestions and ideas from employees for improving the general standards of health and safety at the Company's premises. Consultation with employees via BLANK II (*e.g.* safety representative) will take place from time to time for the purpose of considering suggestions for improvement.

3. Employees' Duties

3.1   This Policy will only be successful if all employees co-operate   **A1–05**
with it. The Company requires all its employees to familiarise themselves with this Policy and to comply with it.

3.2   The Company requires all of its employees to support actions aimed at improving health and safety at work. To this end, the Company expects them to contribute towards creating and maintaining working conditions that are as healthy and safe as reasonably practicable.

3.3   Each employee has a duty under section 7 of the Health & Safety at Work Act 1974:

3.3.1   To take reasonable care for the health and safety for him/herself and of other persons who may be affected by his/her acts and omissions;
and

3.3.2   To co-operate with his/her employer or any other person to perform or comply with a duty or requirement of the health and safety legislation.

3.4   Employers have further duties under regulation 12 of the   **A1–06**
Management of Health and Safety at Work Regulations 1992:

3.4.1   To use any machinery, equipment, dangerous substance or safety device provided by the Company in accordance with any training or instruction given by or on behalf of the Company:

3.4.2   To inform his/her immediate line manager of any serious or imminent danger and to report to that person any shortcomings in the Company's protection arrangements for health and safety at its premises.

3.5   The Company will seek to ensure that its employees are aware of these duties and comply with them.

3.6   Any employees, regardless of status, found to be deliberately and/or consistently negligent in the performance of the Company's Policy on health and safety may be subject to disciplinary proceedings.

4. Management Structure

A1–07   4.1   The overall responsibility for health and safety and for the Policy rests with the Board of Directors.

4.2   The Board of Directors will delegate primary responsibility for the operation and implementation of the Policy to the BLANK III (*e.g.* Managing Director).

4.3   Management at all levels will be responsible to the BLANK III for ensuring the health and safety of those to whom the Policy applies.

4.4   All employees of the Company will be individually responsible for complying with the Policy in accordance with paragraph 3 above.

4.5   The BLANK III will appoint a Safety Committee comprised of BLANK IV.

A1–08   4.6   The Safety Committee will assist in the maintenance of a high standard of health and safety. It will be responsible for:

4.6.1   Discussing the Policy and practices at regular intervals and considering any necessary changes.

4.6.2   Reviewing health and safety issues from time to time and making recommendations to BLANK III for amendment and improvement of the Policy.

4.6.3   Formulating and planning new health and safety policy areas for adoption by the Board of Directors.

4.6.4   Considering reports made to it under paragraph 6 below and recommending appropriate measures to be taken to maintain a safe working environment at the Company's premises.

4.6.5   Devising a suitable health and safety training programme and ensuring it is properly implemented.

4.6.6   Advising generally on health and safety matters.

4.7   Where necessary the Company shall obtain independent specialist advice and services on health and safety matters.

5. Risk Assessment

5.1   In accordance with its duties under regulation 3 of the Management of Health and Safety at Work Regulations 1992 and the Guidance under the Approved Code of Practice 1992, the Company will provide and adopt a programme for the assessment of risks at the Company's premises for the purpose of achieving a high standard of health and safety.   **A1–09**

5.2   The BLANK V (*e.g.* health and safety officer) will be responsible for establishing, implementing and thereafter revising and updating a system to ensure compliance with the Company's Health and Safety Policy and the relevant statutory requirements.

5.3   BLANK V shall ensure that risk assessments are carried out at regular intervals and shall review any assessment if:

5.3.1   There is reason to suspect that it is no longer valid; or

5.3.2   There has been a significant change in the circumstances to which it relates.

A1–10 5.4   The BLANK V shall ensure that the results of the risk assessments are analysed and any appropriate course of action is taken.

5.5   Whilst it remains the responsibility of BLANK V to ensure the necessary action is taken, for the purposes of implementing any changes to the Company's current practice/working conditions, he/she may delegate tasks to suitably competent persons.

5.6   The BLANK V shall ensure that a detailed and up-to-date record is kept of all risk assessments undertaken, the findings and the action taken.

6. Reporting Procedures

A1–11 6.1   The Board of Directors will advise the Safety Committee, BLANK III and all employees of any changes made to the Policy.

6.2   The BLANK III will annually report to the Board of Directors on the working of the Policy during the previous 12 months.

6.3   In accordance with Regulation 8 of the Management of Health and Safety at Work Regulations 1992 BLANK III will be responsible for ensuring that employees are provided with relevant information on the risks to their health and safety as identified by risk assessments and the preventative and protective measures taken to reduce any risks. BLANK V will provide an annual report of all risk assessments undertaken to BLANK III and the Safety Committee, highlighting any hazards revealed and describing the action taken to reduce those hazards. The report may also make suggestions for further improvement to health and safety policy arising out of the risk assessments.

6.4 BLANK V will advise the Safety Committee on all of the **A1–12** following matters at the earliest opportunity after their occurrence:

6.4.1 Accidents resulting in personal injury occurring at the Company's premises;

6.4.2 Incidents occurring at the Company's premises posing a potential threat to the health and safety of the Company's employees or visitors;

6.4.3 Breaches of the Policy or relevant legislation;

6.4.4 Complaints by employees relating to health and safety at work;

6.4.5 Any changes to existing working practices;

6.4.6 The introduction and operation of new technology and equipment;

6.4.7 The introduction and implementation of new health and safety legislation and other relevant statutory provisions.

6.5 BLANK V shall ensure that accidents occurring at the Com- **A1–13** pany's premises are, where necessary, reported in accordance with the Reporting of Injuries Diseases and Dangerous Occurrences Regulations 1995 and also reported to the Safety Committee.

6.6 All employees will be under a duty to report any of the matters listed in paragraph 6.4 to their immediate line manager at the earliest opportunity.

6.7 The Safety Committee will prepare Minutes of all health and safety meetings and provide a copy of those Minutes to the BLANK III. It will report to BLANK III on any health and safety policy suggestions arising out of Safety Committee Meetings.

For and on behalf of the Board
of BLANK COMPANY

Signed: ....
Chairman

Dated: ....

Potential Subject Matter of Supplemental Policies

— Emergency procedures/fire **A1–14**

— Manual handling

— Display screen equipment

— Hazardous substances

— Dealing with contractors

— Permits to work

— Scheme of plant and equipment maintenance

— Reporting of accidents, diseases and dangerous occurrences

— Risk assessment programme

— Provision and use of personal protective equipment

APPENDIX 2

SPECIMEN RISK ASSESSMENT FORMAT

A2–01

Name of Assessor:		Assessment Date:	
Department/Unit:		Area:	Serial No:
Description of Hazard and Associated Risk			
Estimate level of risk			
	Slightly harmful	Harmful	Extremely harmful
Highly unlikely	TRIVIAL RISK	TOLERABLE RISK	MODERATE RISK
Unlikely	TOLERABLE RISK	MODERATE RISK	SUBSTANTIAL RISK
Likely	MODERATE RISK	SUBSTANTIAL RISK	INTOLERABLE RISK
Actions Already Taken/Further Actions Required (See Table 4)			
By Whom:		Target Date:	
Date Completed:		Review Date:	
TO BE RETURNED TO:			

APPENDIX 3

COMMON HAZARDS AND PERSONNEL LIKELY TO BE AFFECTED

Part I—Common Hazards

— Slipping or tripping

A3–01

— Fire

— Chemicals

— Moving parts of machinery

— Working at height

— Vulnerability to falling objects

— Pressure systems

— Vehicles

— Electricity

— Dust and fumes

— Lifting or carrying

— Noise

— Lighting

— Temperature

Part II—Personnel Likely to Be Affected by Hazards

A3–02   — Operatives

— Maintenance and repair personnel

— Contractors

— Cleaners/caterers/security staff

— Trainees

— Lone workers

— People who work off-site

— Members of the public

APPENDIX 4

EXTRACTS FROM JUDGMENTS — ASSESSING CREDIBILITY OF PLAINTIFFS' EVIDENCE

"I accept all the evidence which has been given by Mr John Bai-   **A4–01**
ley".

Caulfield J.
Bailey v. ICI, May 1979, page 2.

"For the purpose of assessing damages, I find the symptoms themselves as described by the Plaintiff as providing the most valuable
guide".

Goff J.
Rollinson v. Thomas C. Wild Ltd, May 1979, page 6.

"I should say that I accept entirely the evidence of Mr Robinson and
Mrs Robinson".

Davies J.
Robinson v. British Rail Engineering Ltd, June 1981, page 3.

"The Court has first the descriptions given by the Plaintiff and his   **A4–02**
wife. I accept these as truthful".

Mustill J.
Heslop v. Metalock (Britain) Ltd, November 1981, page 4.

"I observed both the Plaintiff and his wife in the witness box, I am quite satisfied that neither were given to exaggeration".

Popplewell J.
Kellet v. British Rail Engineering Ltd, May 1984, page 12.

"So far as quantifying this loss is concerned, I am bound to say I accept the Plaintiff's evidence. It was simple, straight-forward and candid and throughout had the ring of truth".

Garland J.
Kay v. James W. Cook (Wivenhoe) Ltd, June 1987, page 5.

APPENDIX 5

DIVISION OF RESPONSIBILITIES BETWEEN HEALTH AND SAFETY EXECUTIVE AND LOCAL AUTHORITIES

Note: The following information is taken from Schedule 1, Health **A5–01** and Safety (Enforcing Authority) Regulations 1989 (S.I. 1989 No. 1903). See the regulations for ancillary provisions and exceptions.

Activities under Local Authority Jurisdiction

1. The sale or storage of goods for retail or wholesale distribu- **A5–02** tion except —

   (a) where it is part of the business of a *transport undertaking*;

   (b) at container depots where the main activity is the storage of goods in the course of transit to or from *dock premises*, an airport or a *railway*;

   (c) where the main activity is the sale or storage for whole-sale distribution of any *dangerous substance*;

(d) where the main activity is the sale or storage of water or sewage or their by-products or natural or town *gas*,

and for the purposes of this paragraph where the main activity carried on in premises is the sale and fitting of motor car tyres, exhausts, windscreens or sunroofs the main activity shall be deemed to be the sale of goods.

A5–03   2. The display or demonstration of goods at an exhibition for the purposes of offer or advertisement for sale.

3. Office activities.

4. Catering services.

5. The provision of permanent or temporary residential accommodation including the provision of a site for caravans or campers.

6. Consumer services provided in a shop except dry cleaning or radio and television repairs, and in this paragraph "consumer services" means services of a type ordinarily supplied to persons who received them otherwise than in the course of a trade, business or other undertaking carried on by them (whether for profit or not).

A5–04   7. Cleaning (wet or dry) in coin operated units in launderettes and similar premises.

8. The use of a bath, sauna or solarium, massaging, hair transplanting, skin piercing, manicuring or other cosmetic services and therapeutic treatments, except where they are carried out under the supervision or control of a registered medical practitioner, a dentist registered under the Dentists Act 1984, a physiotherapist, an osteopath or a chiropractor.

9. The practice or presentation of the arts, sports, games, entertainment or other cultural or recreational activities except where carried on in a museum, art gallery or *theatre* or where the main activity is the exhibition of a cave to the public.

A5–05   10. The hiring out of *pleasure craft* for use on inland waters.

11. The care, treatment, accommodation or exhibition of animals, birds or other creatures, except where the main activity

146

is horse breeding or horse training at a stable, or is an *agricultural activity* or *veterinary surgery*.

12. The activities of an undertaker, except where the main activity is embalming or making of coffins.

13. Church worship or religious meetings.

Activities under H.S.E. Jurisdiction

1. Any activity in a *mine* or *quarry* other than a quarry in respect of which notice of abandonment has been given under section 139(2) of the Mines and Quarries Act 1954. **A5–06**

2. Any activity in a *fairground*.

3. Any activity in premises occupied by a radio, television or film undertaking in which the activity of broadcasting, recording or filming is carried on, and the activity of broadcasting, recording or filming wherever carried on, and for this purpose "film" includes video.

4. The following activities carried on at any premises by persons who do not normally work in the premises — **A5–07**

   (a) *construction work if* —

      (i) section 127(6) of the Factories Act 1961 (which requires certain work to be notified to an inspector) applies to such work; or

      (ii) the whole or part of the work contracted to be undertaken by the *contractor* at the premises is to the external fabric or other external part of a building or structure; or

      (iii) it is carried out in a physically segregated area of the premises, the activities normally carried out in that area have been suspended for the purpose of enabling the *construction work* to be carried out, the *contractor* has authority to exclude from that area persons who are not attending in connection with the carrying out of the work and the work is not the maintenance of insulation of pipes, boilers or other parts of heating or water systems or its removal from them;

(b) the installation, maintenance or repair of any *gas system*, or any work in relation to a *gas fitting*;

(c) the installation, maintenance or repair of *electricity systems*;

(d) work with *ionising radiations* except work in one or more of the categories set out in Schedule 3 to the Ionising Radiations Regulations 1985.

A5–08

5. The use of *ionising radiations* for medical exposure (within the meaning of regulation 2(1) of the Ionising Radiations Regulations 1985).

6. Any activity in premises occupied by a radiography undertaking in which there is carried on any work with *ionising radiations*.

7. *Agricultural activities*, and any activity at an agricultural show which involves the handling of *livestock* or the working of agricultural equipment.

8. Any activity on board a sea-going ship.

9. Any activity in relation to a ski slope, ski lift, ski tow or cable car.

10. Fish, maggot and game breeding except in a *zoo*.

APPENDIX 6

HEALTH AND SAFETY AT WORK ACT 1974, SECTIONS 2 TO 9 AND 37

General Duties

General duties of employers to their employees

2. — (1) It shall be the duty of every employer to ensure, so far as is **A6–01** reasonably practicable, the health, safety and welfare at work of all his employees.

(2) Without prejudice to the generality of an employer's duty under the preceding subsection, the matters to which that duty extends include in particular —

(a) the provision and maintenance of plant and systems of work that are, so far as is reasonably practicable, safe and without risks to health;

(b) arrangements for ensuring, so far as is reasonably practicable, safety and absence of risks to health in connection with the use, handling, storage and transport of articles and substances;

(c) the provision of such information, instruction, training and supervision as is necessary to ensure, so far as is reasonably practicable, the health and safety at work of his employees;

(d) so far as is reasonably practicable, as regards any place of work under the employer's control, the maintenance of it in a condition that is safe and without risks to health and the provision and maintenance of means of access to and egress from it that are safe and without such risks;

(e) the provision and maintenance of a working environment for his employees that is, so far as is reasonably practicable, safe, without risks to health, and adequate as regards facilities and arrangements for their welfare at work.

(3) Except in such cases as may be prescribed, it shall be the duty of every employer to prepare and as often as may be appropriate revise a written statement of his general policy with respect to the health and safety at work of his employees and the organisation and arrangements for the time being in force for carrying out that policy and to bring the statement and any revision of it to the notice of all of his employees.

A6–02   (4) Regulations made by the Secretary of State may provide for the appointment in prescribed cases by recognised trade unions (within the meaning of the regulations) of safety representatives from amongst the employees, and those representatives shall represent the employees in consultations with the employers under subsection (6) below and shall have such other functions as may be prescribed.

(5) [...]

(6) It shall be the duty of every employer to consult any such representatives with a view to the making and maintenance of arrangements which will enable him and his employees to co-operate effectively in promoting and developing measures to ensure the health and safety at work of the employees, and in checking the effectiveness of such measures.

(7) In such cases as may be prescribed it shall be the duty of every employer, if requested to do so by the safety representatives mentioned in [subsection (4)][...] above, to establish, in accordance with regulations made by the Secretary of State, a safety committee having the function of keeping under review the measures taken to ensure the health and safety at work of his employees and such other functions as may be prescribed.

General duties of employers and self-employed to persons other than their employees

3. — (1) It shall be the duty of every employer to conduct his   **A6–03**
undertaking in such a way as to ensure, so far as is reasonably
practicable, that persons not in his employment who may be affected
thereby are not thereby exposed to risks to their health or safety.

(2) It shall be the duty of every self employed person to conduct his
undertaking in such a way as to ensure, so far as is reasonably
practicable, that he and other persons (not being his employees) who
may be affected thereby are not thereby exposed to risks to their
health or safety.

(3) In such cases as may be prescribed, it shall be the duty of every
employer and every self-employed person, in the prescribed circumstances and in the prescribed manner, to give to persons (not being
his employees) who may be affected by the way in which he conducts
his undertaking the prescribed information about such aspects of the
way in which he conducts his undertaking as might affect their health
or safety.

General duties of persons concerned with premises to persons other than their employees

4. — (1) This section has effect for imposing on persons duties in   **A6–04**
relation to those who —

(a)   are not their employees; but

(b)   use non-domestic premises made available to them as a
      place of work or as a place where they may use plant or
      substances provided for their use there,

and applies to premises so made available and other non-domestic
premises used in connection with them.

(2) It shall be the duty of each person who has, to any extent,
control of premises to which this section applies or of the means of
access thereto or egress therefrom or of any plant or substance in

such premises to take such measures as it is reasonable for a person in his position to take to ensure, so far as is reasonably practicable, that the premises, all means of access thereto or egress therefrom available for use by persons using the premises, and any plant or substance in the premises or, as the case may be, provide for use there, is or are safe and without risks to health.

(3) Where a person has, by virtue of any contract or tenancy, an obligation of any extent in relation to —

(a) the maintenance or repair of any premises to which this section applies or any means of access thereto or egress therefrom; or

(b) the safety of or the absence of risks to health arising from plant or substances in any such premises;

that person shall be treated, for the purposes of subsection (2) above, as being a person who has control of the matters to which his obligation extends.

(4) Any reference in this section to a person having control of any premises or matter is a reference to a person having control of the premises or matter in connection with the carrying on by him of a trade, business or other, undertaking (whether for profit or not).

General duty of persons in control of certain premises in relation to harmful emissions into atmosphere

A6–05   5. — (1) [Subject to subsection (5) below,] It shall be the duty of the persons having control of any premises of a class prescribed for the purposes of section 1(1) (d) to use the best practicable means for preventing the emission into the atmosphere, from the premises, of noxious or offensive substances and for rendering harmless and inoffensive such substances as may be so emitted.

(2) The reference in subsection (1) above to the means to be used for the purposes there mentioned includes a reference to the manner in which the plant provided for those purposes is used and to the supervision of any operation involving the emission of the substances to which that subsection applies.

(3) Any substance or a substance of any description prescribed for the purposes of subsection (1) above as noxious or offensive shall be a noxious or, as the case may be, an offensive substance for those purposes whether or not it would be so apart from this subsection.

(4) Any reference in this section to a person having control of any premises is a reference to a person having control of the premises in connection with the carrying on by him of a trade, business or other undertaking (whether, for profit or not) and any duty imposed on any such person by this section shall extend only to matters within his control.

(5) The foregoing provisions of this section shall not apply in relation to any process which is a prescribed process as from the date which is the determination date for that process. **A6–06**

(6) For the purposes of subsection (6) above, the "determination date" for a prescribed process is —

(a) in the case of a process for which an authorisation is granted, the date on which the enforcing authority grants it, whether in pursuance of the application or, on an appeal, of a direction to grant it;

(b) in the case of a process for which an authorisation is refused, the date of refusal or, on an appeal, of the affirmation of the refusal.

(7) In subsections (5) and (6) above "authorisation", "enforcing authority" and "prescribed process" have the meaning given in section 1 of the Environmental Protection Act 1990 and the reference to an appeal is a reference to an appeal under section is of that Act.

General duties of manufacturers, etc. as regards articles and substances for use at work;

6. — (1) It shall be the duty of any person who designs, manufactures, imports or supplies any article for use at work or any article of fairground equipment — **A6–07**

(a) to ensure, so far as is reasonably practicable, that the article is so designed and construed that it will be safe and without risks to health at all times when it is being set, used, cleaned or maintained by a person at work;

(b)   to carry out or arrange for the carrying out of such testing and examination as may be necessary for the performance of the duty imposed on him by the preceding paragraph;

(c)   to take such steps as are necessary to secure that persons supplied by that person with the article are provided with adequate information about the use for which the article is designed or has been tested and about any conditions necessary to ensure that it will be safe and without risks to health at all such times as are mentioned in paragraph (a) above and when it is being dismantled or disposed of; and

(d)   to take such steps as are necessary to secure, so far as is reasonably practicable, that persons so supplied are provided with all such revisions of information provided to them by virtue of the preceding paragraph as are necessary by reason of its becoming known that anything gives rise to a serious risk to health or safety.]

[(1A) It shall be the duty of any person who designs, manufactures, imports or supplies any article of fairground equipment —

(a)   to ensure, so far as is reasonably practicable, that the article is so designed and constructed that it will be safe and without risks to health at all times when it is being used for or in connection with the entertainment of members of the public;

(b)   to carry out or arrange for the carrying out of such testing and examination as may be necessary for the performance of the duty imposed on him by the preceding paragraph;

(c)   to take such steps as are necessary to secure that persons supplied by that person with the article are provided with adequate information about the use for which the article is designed or has been tested and about any conditions necessary to ensure that it will be safe and without risks to health at all times when it is being used for or in connection with the entertainment of members of the public; and

154

(d) to take such steps as are necessary to secure, so far as is reasonably practicable, that persons so supplied are provided with all such revisions of information provided to them by virtue of the preceding paragraph as are necessary by reason of its becoming known that anything gives rise to a serious risk to health or safety.]

(2) It shall be the duty of any person who undertakes the design or manufacture of any article for use at work [or of any article of fairground equipment] to carry out or arrange for the carrying out of any necessary research with a view to the discovery and, so far as is reasonably practicable, the elimination or minimisation of any risks to health or safety to which the design or article may give rise.

(3) It shall be the duty of any person who erects or installs any article for use at work in any premises where that article is to be used by persons at work [or who erects or installs any article of fairground equipment] to ensure, so far as is reasonably practicable, that nothing about the way in which [the article is erected or installed makes it unsafe or a risk to health at such time as is mentioned in paragraph (a) of subsection (1) or, as the case may be, in paragraph (a) of subsection (1) or (1A) above].

[(4) It shall be the duty of any person who manufactures, imports or supplies any substance —

(a) to ensure, so far as is reasonably practicable, that the substance will be safe and without risk to health at all times when it is being used, handled, processed, stored or transported by a person at work or in premises to which section 4 above applies;

(b) to carry out or arrange for the carrying out of such testing and examination as may be necessary for the performance of the duty imposed on him by the preceding paragraph;

(c) to take such steps as are necessary to secure that persons supplied by that person with the substance are provided with adequate information about any risks to health or safety to which the inherent properties of the substance may give rise, about the results of any relevant tests which have been carried out on or in connection with the substance and about any conditions necessary to ensure that the substance will be safe and without risks to health at all

155

such times as are mentioned in paragraph (a) above and when the substance is being disposed of; and

(d) to take such steps as are necessary to secure, so far as is reasonably practicable, that persons so supplied are provided with all such revisions of information provided to them by virtue of the preceding paragraph as are necessary by reason of its becoming known that anything gives rise to a serious risk to health or safety].

A6–09 (5) It shall be the duty of any person who undertakes the manufacture of any [substance] carry out or arrange for the carrying out of any necessary research with a view to the discovery and, so far as is reasonably practicable, the elimination or minimisation of any risks to health or safety to which the substance may give rise [at all such times as are mentioned in paragraph (a) of subsection (4) above].

(6) Nothing in the preceding provisions of this section shall be taken to require a person to repeat any testing, examination or research which has been carried out otherwise than by him or at his instance, in so far as it is reasonable for him to rely on the results thereof for the purposes of those provisions.

(7) Any duty imposed on any person by any of the preceding provisions of this section shall extend only to things done in the course of a trade, business or other undertaking carried on by him (whether for profit or not) and to matters within his control.

(8) Where a person designs, manufactures, imports or supplies an article [for use at work or an article of fairground equipment and does so for or to another] on the basis of a written undertaking by that other to take specified steps sufficient to ensure, so far as is reasonably practicable, that the article will be safe and without risks to health [at all such times as are mentioned in paragraph (a) of subsection (1) or, as the case may be, in paragraph (a) of subsection (1) or (1A) above], the undertaking shall have the effect of relieving the first-mentioned person from the duty imposed [by virtue of that paragraph] to such extent as is reasonable having regard to the terms of the undertaking.

[(8A) Nothing in subsection (7) or (8) above shall relieve any person who imports any article or substance from any duty in respect of anything which —

(a) in the case of an article designed outside the United Kingdom, was done by and in the course of any trade, profession or other undertaking carried on by, or was within the control of, the person who designed the article; or

(b) in the case of an article or substance manufactured outside the United Kingdom, was done by and in the course of any trade, profession or other undertaking carried on by, or was within the control of, the person who manufactured the article or substance.]

(9) Where a person ("the ostensible supplier") supplies any [article or substance] to another ("the customer") under a hire-purchase agreement, conditional sale agreement or credit-sale agreement, and the ostensible supplier — **A6–10**

(a) carries on the business of financing the acquisition of goods by others by means of such agreements; and

(b) in the course of that business acquired his interest in the article or substance supplied to the customer as a means of financing its acquisition by the customer from a third person ("the effective supplier"),

the effective supplier and not the ostensible supplier shall be treated for the purposes of this section as supplying the article or substance to the customer, and any duty imposed by the preceding provisions of this section on suppliers shall accordingly fall on the effective supplier and not on the ostensible supplier.

[(10) For the purposes of this section absence of safety or a risk to health shall be disregarded in so far as the case in or in relation to which it would arise is shown to be one the occurrence of which could not reasonably be foreseen; and in determining whether any duty imposed by virtue of paragraph (a) of subsection (1), (1A) or (4) above has been performed regard shall be had to any relevant information or advice which has been provided to any person by the person by whom the article has been designed, manufactured, imported or supplied or, as the case may be, by the person by whom the substance has been manufactured, imported or supplied.]

General duties of employees at work

A6–11 **7.** It shall be the duty of every employee while at work —

    (a)   to take reasonable care for the health and safety of himself and of other persons who may be affected by his acts or omissions at work; and

    (b)   as regards any duty or requirement imposed on his employer or any other person by or under any of the relevant statutory provisions, to co-operate with him so far as is necessary to enable that duty or requirement to be performed or complied with.

Duty not to interfere with or misuse things provided pursuant to certain provisions

A6–12 **8.** No person shall intentionally or recklessly interfere with or misuse anything provided in the interests of health, safety or welfare in pursuance of any of the relevant statutory provisions.

Duty not to charge employees for things done or provided pursuant to certain specific enactments

A6–13 **9.** No employer shall levy or permit to be levied on any employee of his any charge in respect of anything done or provided in pursuance of any specific requirement of the relevant statutory provisions.

Offences by bodies corporate

A6–14 **37.** — (1) Where an offence under any of the relevant statutory provisions committed by a body corporate is proved to have been

158

committed with the consent or connivance of, or to have been attributable to any neglect on the part of, any director, manager, secretary or other similar officer of the body corporate or a person who was purporting to act in any such capacity, he as well as the body corporate shall be guilty of that offence and shall be liable to be proceeded against and punished accordingly.

(2) Where the affairs of a body corporate are managed by its members, the preceding subsection shall apply in relation to the acts and defaults of a member in connection with his functions of management as if he were a director of the body corporate.

APPENDIX 7

THE MANAGEMENT OF HEALTH AND SAFETY AT WORK REGULATIONS 1992

(S.I. 1992 No. 2051)

Made	*26th August 1992*
Laid before Parliament	*8th September 1992*
Coning into force	*1st January 1993*

ARRANGEMENT OF REGULATIONS

1. Citation, commencement and interpretation. **7–01**

2. Disapplication of these Regulations.

3. Risk assessment.

4. Health and safety arrangements.

5. Health surveillance.

6. Health and safety assistance.

7. Procedures for serious and imminent danger and for danger areas.

8. Information for employees.

9. Co-operation and co-ordination.

10. Persons working in host employers' or self-employed persons' undertakings.

11. Capabilities and training.

12. Employees' duties.

13. Temporary workers.

14. Exemption certificates.

15. Exclusion of civil liability.

16. Extension outside Great Britain.

17. Modification of instrument.
The Schedule.

The Secretary of State, in exercise of the powers conferred upon her by sections 15(1), (2), (5) and (9), 47(2) and 52(2) and (3) of, and paragraphs 6(1), 7, 8(1), 14, 15(1) and 16 of Schedule 3 to, the Health and Safety at Work etc. Act 1974,[1] and of all other powers enabling her in that behalf and for the purpose of giving effect without modifications to proposals submitted to her by the Health and Safety Commission under section 11(2)(d) of the said Act after the carrying out by the said Commission of consultations in accordance with section 50(3) of that Act, hereby makes the following Regulations:

Citation, commencement and interpretation

A7–02   1. — (1) These Regulations may be cited as the Management of Health and Safety at Work Regulations 1992 and shall come into force on 1st January 1993.
(2) In these Regulations —

"the assessment" means, in the case of an employer, the assessment made by him in accordance with regulation 3(1) and changed by him where necessary in accordance with regulation

---

[1] 1974 c.37; sections 15(1), 47(2), 50(3) and 52(3) were amended by the Employment Protection Act 1975 (c.71), Schedule 15, paragraphs 6, 14, 16(3) and 17 respectively.

3(3); and, in the case of a self-employed person, the assessment made by him in accordance with regulation 3(2) and changed by him where necessary in accordance with regulation 3(3);

"employment business" means a business (whether or not carried on with a view to profit and whether or not carried on in conjunction with any other business) which supplies persons (other than seafarers) who are employed in it to work for and under the control of other persons in any capacity;

"fixed-term contract of employment" means a contract of employment for a specific term which is fixed in advance or which can be ascertained in advance by reference to some relevant circumstance; and

"the preventive and protective measures" means the measures which have been identified by the employer or by the self-employed person in consequence of the assessment as the measures he needs to take to comply with the requirements and prohibitions imposed upon him by or under the relevant statutory provisions.

(3) Any reference in these Regulations to —

(a)   a numbered regulation is a reference to the regulation in these Regulations so numbered; or

(b)   a numbered paragraph is a reference to the paragraph so numbered in the regulation in which the reference appears.

Disapplication of these Regulations

2. These Regulations shall not apply to or in relation to the master or crew of a sea-going ship or to the employer of such persons in respect of the normal ship-board activities of a ship's crew under the direction of the master.   **A7–03**

Risk assessment

3. — (1) Every employer shall make a suitable and sufficient assessment of —   **A7–04**

(a)   the risks to the health and safety of his employees to which they are exposed whilst they are at work; and

(b)   the risks to the health and safety of persons not in his employment arising out of or in connection with the conduct by him of his undertaking,

for the purpose of identifying the measures he needs to take to comply with the requirements and prohibitions imposed upon him by or under the relevant statutory provisions.

(2) Every self-employed person shall make a suitable and sufficient assessment of —

(a)   the risks to his own health and safety to which he is exposed whilst he is at work; and

(b)   the risks to the health and safety of persons not in his employment arising out of or in connection with the conduct by him of his undertaking,

for the purpose of identifying the measures he needs to take to comply with the requirements and prohibitions imposed upon him by or under the relevant statutory provisions.

(3) Any assessment such as is referred to in paragraph (1) or (2) shall be reviewed by the employer or self-employed person who made it if —

(a)   there is reason to suspect that it is no longer valid; or

(b)   there has been a significant change in the matters to which it relates;

and where as a result of any such review changes to an assessment are required, the employer or self-employed person concerned shall make them.

(4) Where the employer employs five or more employees, he shall record —

(a)   the significant findings of the assessment; and

(b)   any group of his employees identified by it as being especially at risk.

Health and safety arrangements

4. — (1) Every employer shall make and give effect to such arrange- **A7–05**
ments as are appropriate, having regard to the nature of his activities
and the size of his undertaking, for the effective planning, organisation, control, monitoring and review of the preventive and protective
measures.

(2) Where the employer employs five or more employees, he shall
record the arrangements referred to in paragraph (1).

Health surveillance

5. Every employer shall ensure that his employees are provided with **A7–06**
such health surveillance as is appropriate having regard to the risks to
their health and safety which are identified by the assessment.

Health and safety assistance

6. — (1) Every employer shall, subject to paragraphs (6) and (7), **A7–07**
appoint one or more competent persons to assist him in undertaking
the measures he needs to take to comply with the requirements and
prohibitions imposed upon him by or under the relevant statutory
provisions.

(2) Where an employer appoints persons in accordance with
paragraph (1), he shall make arrangements for ensuring adequate co-
operation between them.

(3) The employer shall ensure that the number of persons appointed under paragraph (1), the time available for them to fulfil their
functions and the means at their disposal are adequate having regard
to the size of his undertaking, the risks to which his employees are
exposed and the distribution of those risks throughout the undertaking.

(4) The employer shall ensure that —

    (a)   any person appointed by him in accordance with para-
            graph (1) who is not in his employment —

     (i)   is informed of the factors known by him to affect, or suspected by him of affecting, the health and safety of any other person who may be affected by the conduct of his undertaking, and

     (ii)   has access to the information referred to in regulation 8; and

  (b)   any person appointed by him in accordance with paragraph (1) is given such information about any person working in his undertaking who is —

     (i)   employed by him under a fixed-term contract of employment, or

     (ii)   employed in an employment business,

as is necessary to enable that person properly to carry out the function specified in that paragraph.

A7–08   (5) A person shall be regarded as competent for the purposes of paragraph (1) where he has sufficient training and experience or knowledge and other qualities to enable him properly to assist in undertaking the measures referred to in that paragraph.

(6) Paragraph (1) shall not apply to a self-employed employer who is not in partnership with any other person where he has sufficient training and experience or knowledge and other qualities properly to undertake the measures referred to in that paragraph himself.

(7) Paragraph (1) shall not apply to individuals who are employers and who are together carrying on business in partnership where at least one of the individuals concerned has sufficient training and experience or knowledge and other qualities —

  (a)   properly to undertake the measures he needs to take to comply with the requirements and prohibitions imposed upon him by or under the relevant statutory provisions; and

  (b)   properly to assist his fellow partners in undertaking the measures they need to take to comploy with the requirements and prohibitions imposed upon them by or under the relevant statutory provisions.

Procedures for serious and imminent danger and for danger areas.

7. — (1) Every employer shall —

    (a)   establish and where necessary give effect to appropriate procedures to be followed in the event of serious and imminent danger to persons at work in his undertaking;

    (b)   nominate a sufficient number of competent persons to implement those procedures insofar as they relate to the evacuation from premises of persons at work in his undertaking; and

    (c)   ensure that none of his employees has access to any area occupied by him to which it is necessary to restrict access on grounds of health and safety unless the employee concerned has received adequate health and safety instruction.

(2) Without prejudice to the generality of paragraph (1)(a), the procedures referred to in that sub-paragraph shall —

    (a)   so far as is practicable, require any persons at work who are exposed to serious and imminent danger to be informed of the nature of the hazard and of the steps taken or to be taken to protect them from it;

    (b)   enable the persons concerned (if necessary by taking appropriate steps in the absence of guidance or instruction and in the light of their knowledge and the technical means at their disposal) to stop work and immediately proceed to a place of safety in the event of their being exposed to serious, imminent and unavoidable danger; and

    (c)   save in exceptional cases for reasons duly substantiated (which cases and reasons shall be specified in those procedures), require the persons concerned to be prevented from resuming work in any situation where there is still a serious and imminent danger.

(3) A person shall be regarded as competent for the purposes of paragraph (1)(b) where he has sufficient training and experience or knowledge and other qualities to enable him properly to implement the evacuation procedures referred to in that sub-paragraph.

Information for employees

A7–10 **8.** Every employer shall provide his employees with comprehensible and relevant information on —

    (a)   the risks to their health and safety identified by the assessment;

    (b)   the preventive and protective measures;

    (c)   the procedures referred to in regulation 7(1)(a);

    (d)   the identity of those persons nominated by him in accordance with regulation 7(1)(b); and

    (e)   the risks notified to him in accordance with regulation 9(1)(c).

Co-operation and co-ordination

A7–11 **9.** — (1) Where two or more employers share a workplace (whether on a temporary or a permanent basis) each such employer shall —

    (a)   co-operate with the other employers concerned so far as is necessary to enable them to comply with the requirements and prohibitions imposed upon them by or under the relevant statutory provisions;

    (b)   (taking into account the nature of his activities) take all reasonable steps to co-ordinate the measures he takes to comply with the requirements and prohibitions imposed upon him by or under the relevant statutory provisions with the measures the other employers concerned are taking to comply with the requirements and prohibitions imposed upon them by or under the relevant statutory provisions; and

(c) take all reasonable steps to inform the other employers concerned of the risks to their employees' health and safety arising out of or in connection with the conduct by him of his undertaking.

(2) Paragraph (1) shall apply to employers sharing a workplace with self-employed persons and to self-employed persons sharing a workplace with other self-employed persons as it applies to employers sharing a workplace with other employers; and the references in that paragraph to employers and the reference in the said paragraph to their employees shall be construed accordingly.

Persons working in host employers' or self-employed persons' undertakings

10. — (1) Every employer and every self-employed person shall ensure that the employer of any employees from an outside undertaking who are working in his undertaking is provided with comprehensible information on — **A7–12**

(a) the risks to those employees' health and safety arising out of or in connection with the conduct by that first-mentioned employer or by that self-employed person of his undertaking; and

(b) the measures taken by that first-mentioned employer or by that self-employed person in compliance with the requirements and prohibitions imposed upon him by or under the relevant statutory provisions insofar as the said requirements and prohibitions relate to those employees.

(2) Paragraph (1) shall apply to a self-employed person who is working in the undertaking of an employer or a self-employed person as it applies to employees from an outside undertaking who are working therein; and the reference in that paragraph to the employer of any employees from an outside undertaking who are working in the undertaking of an employer or a self-employed person and the references in the said paragraph to employees from an outside undertaking who are working in the undertaking of an employer or a self-employed person shall be construed accordingly.

(3) Every employer shall ensure that any person working in his undertaking who is not his employee and every self-employed person (not being an employer) shall ensure that any person working in his undertaking is provided with appropriate instructions and comprehensible information regarding any risks to that person's health and safety which arise out of the conduct by that employer or self-employed person of his undertaking.

(4) Every employer shall —

(a) ensure that the employer of any employees from an outside undertaking who are working in his undertaking is provided with sufficient information to enable that second-mentioned employer to identify any person nominated by that first-mentioned employer in accordance with regulation 7(1)(b) to implement evacuation procedures as far as those employees are concerned; and

(b) take all reasonable steps to ensure that any employees from an outside undertaking who are working in his undertaking receive sufficient information to enable them to identify any person nominated by him in accordance with regulation 7(1)(b) to implement evacuation procedures as far as they are concerned.

(5) Paragraph (4) shall apply to a self-employed person who is working in an employer's undertaking as it applies to employees from an outside undertaking who are working therein; and the reference in that paragraph to the employer of any employees from an outside undertaking who are working in an employer's undertaking and the references in the said paragraph to employees from an outside undertaking who are working in an employer's undertaking shall be construed accordingly.

Capabilities and training

11. — (1) Every employer shall, in entrusting tasks to his employees, **A7–13** take into account their capabilities as regards health and safety.

(2) Every employer shall ensure that his employees are provided with adequate health and safety training —

(a) on their being recruited into the employer's undertaking; and

(b) on their being exposed to new or increased risks because of —

(i) their being transferred or given a change of responsibilities within the employer's undertaking,

(ii) the introduction of new work equipment into or a change respecting work equipment already in use within the employer's undertaking,

(iii) the introduction of new technology into the employer's undertaking, or

(iv) the introduction of a new system of work into or a change respecting a system of work already in use within the employer's undertaking.

(3) The training referred to in paragraph (2) shall —

(a) be repeated periodically where appropriate;

(b) be adapted to take account of any new or changed risks to the health and safety of the employees concerned; and

(c) take place during working hours.

Employees' duties

12. — (1) Every employee shall use any machinery, equipment, **A7–14** dangerous substance, transport equipment, means of production or safety device provided to him by his employer in accordance both with any training in the use of the equipment concerned which has been received by him and the instructions respecting that use which have been provided to him by the said employer in compliance with the requirements and prohibitions imposed upon that employer by or under the relevant statutory provisions.

(2) Every employee shall inform his employer or any other employee of that employer with specific responsibility for the health and safety of his fellow employees —

(a) of any work situation which a person with the first-mentioned employee's training and instruction would reasonably consider represented a serious and immediate danger to health and safety; and

(b) of any matter which a person with the first-mentioned employee's training and instruction would reasonably consider represented a shortcoming in the employer's protection arrangements for health and safety; and

insofar as that situation or matter either affects the health and safety of that first-mentioned employee or arises out of or in connection with his own activities at work, and has not previously been reported to his employer or to any other employee of that employer in accordance with this paragraph.

Temporary workers

A7–15   **13.** — (1) Every employer shall provide any person whom he has employed under a fixed-term contract of employment with comprehensible information on —

(a) any special occupational qualifications or skills required to be held by that employee if he is to carry out his work safely; and

(b) any health surveillance required to be provided to that employee by or under any of the relevant statutory provisions and shall provide the said information before the employee concerned commences his duties.

(2) Every employer and every self-employed person shall provide any person employed in an employment business who is to carry out work in his undertaking with comprehensible information on —

(a) any special occupational qualifications or skills required to be held by that employee if he is to carry out his work safely; and

(b) any health surveillance required to be provided to that employee by or under any of the relevant statutory provisions.

(3) Every employer and every self-employed person shall ensure that every person carrying on an employment business whose employees are to carry out work in his undertaking is provided with comprehensible information on —

(a) any special occupational qualifications or skills required to be held by those employees if they are to carry out their work safely; and

(b) the specific features of the jobs to be filled by those employees (insofar as those features are likely to affect their health and safety);

and the person carrying on the employment business concerned shall ensure that the information so provided is given to the said employees.

Exemption certificates

14. — (1) The Secretary of State for Defence may, in the interests of national security, by a certificate in writing exempt —   **A7–16**

(a) any of the home forces, any visiting force or any head-quarters from those requirements of these Regulations which impose obligations on employers; or

(b)   any member of the home forces, any member of a visiting force or any member of a headquarters from the requirements imposed by regulation 12;

and any exemption such as is specified in sub-paragraph (a) or (b) of this paragraph may be granted subject to conditions and to a limit of time and may be revoked by the said Secretary of State by a further certificate in writing at any time.

(2) In this regulation —

(a)   "the home forces" has the same meaning as in section 12(1) of the Visiting Forces Act 1952[2];

(b)   "headquarters" has the same meaning as in article 3(2) of the Visiting Forces and International Headquarters (Application of Law) Order 1965[3];

(c)   "member of a headquarters" has the same meaning as in paragraph 1(1) of the Schedule to the International Headquarters and Defence Organisations Act 1964[4]; and

(d)   "visiting force" has the same meaning as it does for the purposes of any provision of Part I of the Visiting Forces Act 1952.

Exclusion of civil liability

A7–17   **15.** Breach of a duty imposed by these Regulations shall not confer a right of action in any civil proceedings.

Extension outside Great Britain

A7–18   **16.** — (1) These Regulations shall, subject to regulation 2, apply to and in relation to the premises and activities outside Great Britain to

---

[2]1952 c.67.
[3]S.I. 1965/1536, to which there are amendments not relevant to these Regulations.
[4]1964 c.5.

which sections 1 to 59 and 80 to 82 of the Health and Safety at Work etc. Act 1974 apply by virtue of the Health and Safety at Work etc. Act 1974 (Application Outside Great Britain) Order 1989[5] as they apply within Great Britain.

(2) For the purposes of Part I of the 1974 Act, the meaning of "at work" shall be extended so that an employee or a self-employed person shall be treated as being at work throughout the time that he is present at the premises to and in relation to which these Regulations apply by virtue of paragraph (1); and, in that connection, these Regulations shall have effect subject to the extension effected by this paragraph.

Modification of instrument

17. The Safety Representatives and Safety Committees Regulations 1977[6] shall be modified to the extent specified in the Schedule to these Regulations.   **A7–19**

THE SCHEDULE   Regulation 17

The following regulation shall be inserted after regulation 4 of the Safety Representatives and Safety Committees Regulations 1977 —   **A7–20**

"Employer's duty to consult and provide facilities and assistance

4A. — (1) Without prejudice to the generality of section 2(6) of the Health and Safety at Work etc. Act 1974, every employer shall consult safety representatives in good time with regard to —

(a) the introduction of any measure at the workplace which may substantially affect the health and safety of the employees the safety representatives concerned represent;

---

[5]S.I. 1989/840.
[6]S.I. 1977/500.

(b)   his arrangements for appointing or, as the case may be, nominating persons in accordance with regulations 6(1) and 7(1)(b) of the Management of Health and Safety at Work Regulations 1992;

(c)   any health and safety information he is required to provide to the employees the safety representatives concerned represent by or under the relevant statutory provisions;

(d)   the planning and organisation of any health and safety training he is required to provide to the employees the safety representatives concerned represent by or under the relevant statutory provisions; and

(e)   the health and safety consequences for the employees the safety representatives concerned represent of the introduction (including the planning thereof) of new technologies into the workplace.

(2) Without prejudice to regulations 5 and 6 of these Regulations, every employer shall provide such facilities and assistance as safety representatives may reasonably require for the purpose of carrying out their functions under section 2(4) of the 1974 Act and under these Regulations.".

APPENDIX 8

THE WORKPLACE (HEALTH, SAFETY AND WELFARE) REGULATIONS 1992

(S.I. 1992 No. 3004)

Made	*1st December 1992*
Laid before Parliament	*8th December 1992*
Coming into force	
The whole Regulations except regulations 5 to 27 and the Schedules, to the extent specified in regulation 1(3)	*1st January 1993*
Regulations 5 to 27 and the Schedules, to the extent specified in regulation 1(3)	*1st January 1996*

The effect of the revocations in Schedule 2 is modified by SI 1993/2482 which is reprinted at the end of this instrument.

ARRANGEMENT OF REGULATIONS

The Secretary of State, in exercise of the powers conferred on her by sections 15(1), (2), (3)(a) and (5)(b), and 82(3)(a) of, and paragraphs 1(2), 9 and 10 of Schedule 3 to, the Health and Safety at Work etc. Act 1974[1] ("the 1974 Act") and of all other powers enabling her in that behalf and for the purpose of giving effect without modifications to proposals submitted to her by the Health and Safety Commission under section 11(2)(d) of the 1974 Act after the carrying out by the said Commission of consultations in accordance with section 50(3) of that Act, hereby makes the following Regulations: —

Citation and commencement

1. — (1) These Regulations may be cited as the Workplace (Health,   **A8–02**
Safety and Welfare)
(2) Subject to paragraph (3), these Regulations shall come into force on 1st January 1993.
(3) Regulations 5 to 27 and the Schedules shall come into force on 1st January 1996 with respect to any workplace or part of a workplace which is not —

(a)   a new workplace; or

(b)   a modification, an extension or a conversion.

---

[1]1974 c.37; sections 15 and 50 were amended by the Employment Protection Act 1975 (c.71), Schedule 15, paragraphs 6 and 16 respectively.

Interpretation

A8–03 **2.** — (1) In these Regulations, unless the context otherwise requires —

"new workplace" means a workplace used for the first time as a workplace after 31st December 1992;

"public road" means (in England and Wales) a highway maintainable at public expense within the meaning of section 329 of the Highways Act 1980[2] and (in Scotland) a public road within the meaning assigned to that term by section 151 of the Roads (Scotland) Act 1984[3];

"traffic route" means a route for pedestrian traffic, vehicles or both and includes any stairs, staircase, fixed ladder, doorway, gateway, loading bay or ramp;

"workplace" means, subject to paragraph (2), any premises or part of premises which are not domestic premises and are made available to any person as a place of work, and includes —

(a) any place within the premises to which such person has access while at work; and

(b) any room, lobby, corridor, staircase, road or other place used as a means of access to or egress from that place of work or where facilities are provided for use in connection with the place of work other than a public road;

but shall not include a modification; an extension or a conversion of any of the above until such modification, extension or conversion is completed.

(2) Any reference in these Regulations, except in paragraph (1), to a modification, an extension or a conversion is a reference, as the case may be, to a modification, an extension or a conversion of a workplace started after 31st December 1992.

(3) Any requirement that anything done or provided in pursuance of these Regulations shall be suitable shall be construed to include a requirement that it is suitable for any person in respect of whom such thing is so done or provided.

(4) Any reference in these Regulations to —

---

[2] 1980 c.66.
[3] 1984 c.54.

(a) a numbered regulation or Schedule is a reference to the regulation in or Schedule to these Regulations so numbered; and

(b) a numbered paragraph is a reference to the paragraph so numbered in the regulation in which the reference appears.

Application of these Regulations

3. — (1) These Regulations apply to every workplace but shall not apply to —   **A8–04**

(a) a workplace which is or is in or on a ship within the meaning assigned to that word by regulation 2(1) of the Docks Regulations 1988[4];

(b) a workplace where the only activities being undertaken are building operations or works of engineering construction within, in either case, section 176 of the Factories Act 1961[5] and activities for the purpose of or in connection with the first-mentioned activities;

(c) a workplace where the only activities being undertaken are the exploration for or extraction of mineral resources; or

(d) a workplace which is situated in the immediate vicinity of another workplace or intended workplace where exploration for or extraction of mineral resources is being or will be undertaken, and where the only activities being undertaken are activities preparatory to, for the purposes of, or in connection with such exploration for or extraction of mineral resources at that other workplace.

(2) In their application to temporary work sites, any requirement to ensure a workplace complies with any of regulations 20 to 25 shall

---

[4]S.I. 1988/1655.
[5]1961 c.34; section 176 has been extended by S.I. 1960/421 and 1968/1530.

have effect as a requirement to so ensure so far as is reasonably practicable.

(3) As respects any workplace which is or is in or on an aircraft, locomotive or rolling stock, trailer or semi-trailer used as a means of transport or a vehicle for which a licence is in force under the Vehicles (Excise) Act 1971[6] or a vehicle exempted from duty under that Act —

(a)   regulations 5 to 12 and 14 to 25 shall not apply to any such workplace; and

(b)   regulation 13 shall apply to any such workplace only when the aircraft, locomotive or rolling stock, trailer or semi-trailer or vehicle is stationary inside a workplace and, in the case of a vehicle for which a licence is in force under the Vehicles (Excise) Act 1971, is not on a public road.

(4) As respects any workplace which is in fields, woods or other land forming part of an agricultural or forestry undertaking but which is not inside a building and is situated away from the under-taking's main buildings —

(a)   regulations 5 to 19 and 23 to 25 shall not apply to any such workplace; and

(b)   any requirement to ensure that any such workplace complies with any of regulations 20 to 22 shall have effect as a requirement to so ensure so far as is reasonably practicable.

Requirements under these Regulations

A8–05   **4.** — (1) Every employer shall ensure that every workplace, modification, extension or conversion which is under his control and where any of his employees works complies with any requirement of these Regulations which —

---

[6]1971 c.10.

(a)   applies to that workplace or, as the case may be, to the workplace which contains that modification, extension or conversion; and

(b)   is in force in respect of the workplace, modification, extension or conversion.

(2) Subject to paragraph (4), every person who has, to any extent, control of a workplace, modification, extension or conversion shall ensure that such workplace, modification, extension or conversion complies with any requirement of these Regulations which —

(a)   applies to that workplace or, as the case may be, to the workplace which contains that modification, extension or conversion:

(b)   is in force in respect of the workplace, modification, extension, or conversion; and

(c)   relates to matters within that person's control.

(3) Any reference in this regulation to a person having control of any workplace, modification, extension or conversion is a reference to a person having control of the workplace, modification, extension or conversion in connection with the carrying on by him of a trade, business or other undertaking (whether for profit or not).

(4) Paragraph (2) shall not impose any requirement upon a self-employed person in respect of his own work or the work of any partner of his in the undertaking.

(5) Every person who is deemed to be the occupier of a factory by virtue of section 175(5) of the Factories Act 1961 shall ensure that the premises which are so deemed to be a factory comply with these Regulations.

Maintenance of workplace, and of equipment, devices and systems

5. — (1) The workplace and the equipment, devices and systems to   **A8–06**
which this regulation applies shall be maintained (including cleaned

183

as appropriate) in an efficient state, in efficient working order and in good repair.

(2) Where appropriate, the equipment, devices and systems to which this regulation applies shall be subject to a suitable system of maintenance.

(3) The equipment, devices and systems to which this regulation applies are —

    (a)   equipment and devices a fault in which is liable to result in a failure to comply with any of these Regulations; and

    (b)   mechanical ventilation systems provided pursuant to regulation 6 (whether or not they include equipment or devices within sub-paragraph (a) of this paragraph).

Ventilation

A8–07   **6.** — (1) Effective and suitable provision shall be made to ensure that every enclosed workplace is ventilated by a sufficient quantity or fresh or purified air.

(2) Any plant used for the purpose of complying with paragraph (1) shall include an effective device to give visible or audible warning of any failure of the plant where necessary for reasons of health or safety

(3) This regulation shall not apply to any enclosed workplace or part of a workplace which is subject to the provisions of —

    (a)   section 30 of the Factories Act 1961[7];

    (b)   regulations 49 to 52 of the Shipbuilding and Ship-Repairing Regulations 1960[8];

    (c)   regulation 21 of the Construction (General Provisions) Regulations 1961[9];

---

[7]1961 c.34; section 30 is amended by S.I. 1983/978.
[8]S.I. 1960/1932.
[9]S.I. 1961/1580, to which there are amendments not relevant to these Regulations.

(d)   regulation 18 of the Docks Regulations 1988[10];

Temperature in indoor workplaces

7. — (1) During working hours, the temperature in all workplaces   **A8–08**
inside buildings shall be reasonable.

(2) A method of heating or cooling shall not be used which results
in the escape into a workplace of fumes, gas or vapour of such
character and to such extent that they are likely to be injurious or
offensive to any person.

(3) A sufficient number of thermometers shall be provided to
enable persons at work to determine the temperature in any workplace inside a building.

Lighting

8. — (1) Every workplace shall have suitable and sufficient lighting.   **A8–09**

(2) The lighting mentioned in paragraph (1) shall, so far as is
reasonably practicable, be by natural light.

(3) Without prejudice to the generality of paragraph (1), suitable
and sufficient emergency lighting shall be provided in any room in
circumstances in which persons at work are specially exposed to
danger in the event of failure of artificial lighting.

Cleanliness and waste materials

9. — (1) Every workplace and the furniture, furnishings and fittings   **A8–10**
there in shall be kept sufficiently clean.

(2) The surfaces of the floors, walls and ceilings of all workplaces
inside buildings shall be capable of being kept sufficiently clean.

---

[10]S.I. 1988/1655.

(3) So far as is reasonably practicable, waste materials shall not be allowed to accumulate in a workplace except in suitable receptacles.

Room dimensions and space

A8–11 **10.** — (1) Every room where persons work shall have sufficient floor area, height and unoccupied space for purposes of health, safety and welfare.

(2) It shall be sufficient compliance with this regulation in a workplace which is not a new workplace, a modification, an extension or a conversion and which, immediately before this regulation came into force in respect of it, was subject to the provisions of the Factories Act 1961, if the workplace does not contravene the provisions of Part I of Schedule 1.

Workstations and seating

A8–12 **11.** — (1) Every workstation shall be so arranged that it is suitable both for any person at work in the workplace who is likely to work at that workstation and for any work of the undertaking which is likely to be done there.

(2) Without prejudice to the generality of paragraph (1), every workstation outdoors shall be so arranged that —

(a) so far as is reasonably practicable, it provides protection from adverse weather;

(b) it enables any person at the workstation to leave it swiftly or, as appropriate, to be assisted in the event of an emergency; and

(c) it ensures that any person at the workstation is not likely to slip or fall.

(3) A suitable seat shall be provided for each person at work in the workplace whose work includes operations of a kind that the work (or a substantial part of it) can or must be done sitting.

(4) A seat shall not be suitable for the purpose of paragraph (3) unless —

(a) it is suitable for the person for whom it is provided as well as for the operations to be performed; and

(b) a suitable footrest is also provided where necessary.

Condition of floors and traffic routes

12. — (1) Every floor in a workplace and the surface of every traffic route in a workplace shall be of a construction such that the floor or surface of the traffic route is suitable for the purpose for which it is used. **A8–13**

(2) Without prejudice to the generality of paragraph (1), the requirements in that paragraph shall include requirements that —

(a) the floor, or surface of the traffic route, shall have no hole or slope, or be uneven or slippery so as, in each case, to expose any person to a risk to his health or safety; and

(b) every such floor shall have effective means of drainage where necessary.

(3) So far as is reasonably practicable, every floor in a workplace and the surface of every traffic route in a workplace shall be kept free from obstructions and from any article or substance which may cause a person to slip, trip or fall.

(4) In considering whether for the purposes of paragraph (2)(a) a hole or slope exposes any person to a risk to his health or safety —

(a) no account shall be taken of a hole where adequate measures have been taken to prevent a person falling; and

(b) account shall be taken of any handrail provided in connection with any slope.

(5) Suitable and sufficient handrails and, if appropriate, guards shall be provided on all traffic routes which are staircases except in

circumstances in which a handrail can not be provided without obstructing the traffic route.

Fall or falling objects

A8–14 **13.** — (1) So far as is reasonably practicable, suitable and effective measures shall be taken to prevent any event specified in paragraph (3).

(2) So far as is reasonably practicable, the measures required by paragraph (1) shall be measures other than the provision of personal protective equipment, information, instruction, training or supervision.

(3) The events specified in this paragraph are —

(a) any person falling a distance likely to cause personal injury;

(b) any person being struck by a falling object likely to cause personal injury.

(4) Any area where there is a risk to health or safety from any event mentioned in paragraph (3) shall be clearly indicated where appropriate.

(5) So far as is practicable, every tank, pit or structure where there is a risk of a person in the workplace falling into a dangerous substance in the tank, pit or structure, shall be securely covered or fenced.

(6) Every traffic route over, across or in an uncovered tank, pit or structure such as is mentioned in paragraph (5) shall be securely fenced.

(7) In this regulation, "dangerous substance" means —

(a) any substance likely to scald or burn;

(b) any poisonous substance;

(c) any corrosive substance;

(d) any fume, gas or vapour likely to overcome a person; or

(e)   any granular or free-flowing solid substance, or any viscous substance which, in any case, is of a nature or quantity which is likely to cause danger to any person.

Windows, and transparent or translucent doors, gates and walls

14. — (1) Every window or other transparent or translucent surface   **A8–15**
in a wall or partition and every transparent or translucent surface in a door or gate shall, where necessary for reasons of health or safety —

(a)   be of safety material or be protected against breakage of the transparent or translucent material; and

(b)   be appropriately marked or incorporate features so as, in either case, to make it apparent.

Windows, skylights and ventilators

15. — (1) No window, skylight or ventilator which is capable of being   **A8–16**
opened shall be likely to be opened, closed or adjusted in a manner which exposes any person performing such operation to a risk to his health or safety.

(2) No window, skylight or ventilator shall be in a position when open which is likely to expose any person in the workplace to a risk to his health or safety.

Ability to clean windows etc. safely

16. — (1) All windows and skylights in a workplace shall be of a   **A8–17**
design or be so constructed that they may be cleaned safely.

189

(2) In considering whether a window or skylight is of a design or so constructed as to comply with paragraph (1), account may be taken of equipment used in conjunction with the window or skylight or of devices fitted to the building.

Organisation etc. of traffic routes

A8–18 **17.** — (1) Every workplace shall be organised in such a way that pedestrians and vehicles can circulate in a safe manner.

(2) Traffic routes in a workplace shall be suitable for the persons or vehicles using them, sufficient in number, in suitable positions and of sufficient size.

(3) Without prejudice to the generality of paragraph (2), traffic routes shall not satisfy the requirements of that paragraph unless suitable measures are taken to ensure that —

(a) pedestrians or, as the case may be, vehicles may use a traffic route without causing danger to the health or safety of persons at work near it;

(b) there is sufficient separation of any traffic route for vehicles from doors or gates or from traffic routes for pedestrians which lead onto it; and

(c) where vehicles and pedestrians use the same traffic route, there is sufficient separation between them.

(4) All traffic routes shall be suitably indicated where necessary for reasons of health or safety.

(5) Paragraph (2) shall apply so far as is reasonably practicable, to a workplace which is not a new workplace, a modification, an extension or a conversion.

Doors and gates

A8–19 **18.** — (1) Doors and gates shall be suitably constructed (including being fitted with any necessary safety devices).

(2) Without prejudice to the generality of paragraph (1), doors and gates shall not comply with that paragraph unless —

(a) any sliding door or gate has a device to prevent coming off its track during use;

(b) any upward opening door or gate has a device to prevent it falling back;

(c) any powered door or gate has suitable and effective features to prevent it causing injury by trapping any person;

(d) where necessary for reasons of health or safety, any powered door or gate can be operated manually unless it, opens automatically if the power fails; and

(e) any door or gate which is capable of opening by being pushed from either side is of such a construction as to provide, when closed, a clear view of the space close to both sides.

Escalators and moving walkways

19. Escalators and moving walkways shall: **A8–20**

(a) function safely;

(b) be equipped with any necessary safety devices;

(c) be fitted with one or more emergency stop controls which are easily identifiable and readily accessible.

Sanitary conveniences

20. — (1) Suitable and sufficient sanitary conveniences shall be   **A8–21** provided at readily accessible places.

(2) Without prejudice to the generality of paragraph (1), sanitary conveniences shall not be suitable unless —

(a) the rooms containing them are adequately ventilated and lit;

(b) they and the rooms containing them are kept in a clean and orderly condition; and

(c) separate rooms containing conveniences are provided for men and women except where and so far as each convenience is in a separate room the door of which is capable of being secured from inside.

(3) It shall be sufficient compliance with the requirement in paragraph (1) to provide sufficient sanitary conveniences in a workplace which is not a new workplace, a modification, an extension or a conversion and which, immediately before this regulation came into force in respect of it, was subject to the provisions of the Factories Act 1961, if sanitary conveniences are provided in accordance with the provisions of Part II of Schedule 1.

Washing facilities

A8–22 **21.** — (1) Suitable and sufficient washing facilities, including showers if required by the nature of the work or for health reasons, shall be provided at readily accessible places.

(2) Without prejudice to the generality of paragraph (1), washing facilities shall not be suitable unless —

(a) they are provided in the immediate vicinity of every sanitary convenience, whether or not provided elsewhere as well;

(b) they are provided in the vicinity of any changing rooms required by these Regulations, whether or not provided elsewhere as well;

(c) they include a supply of clean hot and cold, or warm, water (which shall be running water so far as is practicable);

(d) they include soap or other suitable means of cleaning;

(e) they include towels or other suitable means of drying;

(f)   the rooms containing them are sufficiently ventilated and lit;

(g)   they and the rooms containing them are kept in a clean and orderly condition; and

(h)   separate facilities are provided for men and women, except where and so far as they are provided in a room the door of which is capable of being secured from inside and the facilities in each such room are intended to be used by only one person at a time.

(3) Paragraph (2)(h) shall not apply to facilities which are provided for washing hands, forearms and face only.

Drinking water

22. — (1) An adequate supply of wholesome drinking water shall be provided for all persons at work in the workplace.   **A8–23**
(2) Every supply of drinking water required by paragraph (1) shall —

(a)   be readily accessible at suitable places; and

(b)   be conspicuously marked by an appropriate sign where necessary for reasons of health or safety.

(3) Where a supply of drinking water is required by paragraph (1), there shall also be provided a sufficient number of suitable cups or other drinking vessels unless the supply of drinking water is in a jet from which persons can drink easily.

Accommodation for clothing

23. — (1) Suitable and sufficient accommodation shall be provided —   **A8–24**

(a)   for the clothing of any person at work which is not worn during working hours; and

193

(b)   for special clothing which is worn by any person at work but which is not taken home.

(2) Without prejudice to the generality of paragraph (1), the accommodation mentioned in that paragraph shall not be suitable unless —

(a)   where facilities to change clothing are required by regulation 24, it provides suitable security for the clothing mentioned in paragraph (1)(a);

(b)   where necessary to avoid risks to health or damage to the clothing, it includes separate accommodation for clothing worn at work and for other clothing;

(c)   so far as is reasonably practicable, it allows or includes facilities for drying clothing; and

(d)   it is in a suitable location.

Facilities for changing clothing

A8–25   **24.** — (1) Suitable and sufficient facilities shall be provided for any person at work in the workplace to change clothing in all cases where —

(a)   the person has to wear special clothing for the purpose of work; and

(b)   the person can not, for reasons of health or propriety, be expected to change in another room.

(2) Without prejudice to the generality of paragraph (1), the facilities mentioned in that paragraph shall not be suitable unless they include separate facilities for, or separate use of facilities by, men and women where necessary for reasons of propriety.

Facilities for rest and to eat meals

25. — (1) Suitable and sufficient rest facilities shall be provided at   **A8–26**
readily accessible places.

(2) Rest facilities provided by virtue of paragraph (1) shall —

    (a)   where necessary for reasons of health or safety include, in
the case of a new workplace, an extension or a conversion,
rest facilities provided in one or more rest rooms, or, in
other cases, in rest rooms or rest areas;

    (b)   include suitable facilities to eat meals where food eaten in
the workplace would otherwise be likely to become con-
taminated.

(3) Rest rooms and rest areas shall include suitable arrangements
to protect non-smokers from discomfort caused by tobacco smoke.

(4) Suitable facilities shall be provided for any person at work who
is a pregnant woman or nursing mother to rest.

(5) Suitable and sufficient facilities shall be provided or persons at
work to eat meals where meals are regularly eaten in the workplace.

Exemption certificates

26. — (1) The Secretary of State for Defence may, in the interests of   **A8–27**
national security, by a certificate in writing exempt any of the home
forces, any visiting force or any headquarters from the requirements
of these Regulations and any exemption may be granted subject to
conditions and to a limit of time and may be revoked by the said
Secretary of State by a further certificate in writing at any time.

(2) In this regulation —

    (a)   "the home forces" has the same meaning as in section
12(1) of the Visiting Forces Act 1952[11];

---

[11]1952 c.67.

(b) "headquarters" has the same meaning as in article 3(2) of the Visiting Forces and International Headquarters (Application of Law) Order 1965[12];

(c) "visiting force" has the same meaning as it does for the purposes of any provision of Part I of the Visiting Forces Act 1952.

Repeals, saving and revocations

A8–28 **27.** — (1) The enactments mentioned in column 2 of Part I of Schedule 2 are repealed to the extent specified in column 3 of that Part.

(2) Nothing in this regulation shall affect the operation of any provision of the Offices, Shops and Railway Premises Act 1963[13] as that provision has effect by virtue of section 90(4) of that Act.

(3) The instruments mentioned in column 1 of Part II of Schedule 2 are revoked to the extent specified in column 3 of that Part.

SCHEDULE 1 Regulations 10 and 20
PROVISIONS APPLICABLE TO FACTORIES WHICH ARE NOT NEW WORKPLACES, MODIFICATIONS, EXTENSIONS OR CONVERSIONS

PART 1

SPACE

A8–29 **1.** No room in the workplace shall be so overcrowded as to cause risk to the health or safety of persons at work in it.

---

[12]S.I. 1965/1536, to which there are amendments not relevant to these Regulations.
[13]1963 c.41.

2. Without prejudice to the generality of paragraph 1, the number of persons employed at a time in any workroom shall not be such that the amount of cubic space allowed for each is less than 11 cubic metres.

3. In calculating for the purposes of this Part of this Schedule the amount of cubic space in any room no space more than 4.2 metres from the floor shall be taken into account and, where a room contains a gallery, the gallery shall be treated for the purposes of this Schedule as if it were partitioned off from the remainder of the room and formed a separate room.

PART 2

NUMBER OF SANITARY CONVENIENCES

4. In workplaces where females work, there shall be at least one **A8–30** suitable water closet for use by females only for every 25 females.

5. In workplaces where males work, there shall be at least one suitable water closet for use by males only for every 25 males.

6. In calculating the number of males or females who work in any workplace for the purposes of this Part of this Schedule, any number not itself divisible by 25 without fraction or remainder shall be treated as the next number higher than it which is so divisible.

SCHEDULE 2 — Regulation 27
REPEALS AND REVOCATIONS

PART 1

REPEALS

A8–31

1 Chapter	2 Short title	3 Extent of repeal
1961 c.34	The Factories Act 1961	Sections 1 to 7, 18, 28, 29, 57 to 60 and 69
1963 c.41	The Offices, Shops and Railway Premises Act 1963	Sections 4 to 16
1956 c.49	The Agriculture (Safety, Health and Welfare Provisions) Act 1956	Sections 3 and 5 and, in section 25, sub-sections (3) and (6)

PART 2

REVOCATIONS

(1) Title	(2) Reference	(3) Extent of revocation
The Flax and Tow Spinning and Weaving Regulations 1906	S.R. & O. 1906/177, amended by S.I. 1988/1657	Regulation 3, 8, 10, 11 and 14
The Hemp Spinning and Weaving Regulations 1907	S.R. & O. 1907/660, amended by S.I. 1988/1657	Regulations 3 to 5 and 8

(1) Title	(2) Reference	(3) Extent of revocation
Order dated 5 October 1917 (the Tin or Terne Plates Manufacture Welfare Order 1917)	S.R. & O. 1917/1035	The whole Order
Order dated 15 May 1918 (the Glass Bottle, etc. Manufacture Welfare Order 1918)	S.R. & O. 1918/558	The whole Order
Order dated 15 August 1919 (the Fruit Preserving Welfare Order 1919)	S.R. & O. 1919/1136, amended by S.I. 1988/1657	The whole Order
Order dated 23 April 1920 (the Laundries Welfare Order 1920)	S.R. & O. 1920/654	The whole Order
Order dated 28 July 1920 (the Gut Scraping, Tripe Dressing, etc. Welfare Order 1920)	S.R. & O. 1920/1437	The whole Order
Order dated 9 September 1920 (the Herring Curing (Norfolk and Suffolk) Welfare Order 1920)	S.R. & O. 1920/1662	The whole Order
Order dated 3 March 1921 (the Glass Bevelling Welfare Order 1921)	S.R. & O. 1921/288	The whole Order
The Herring Curing (Scotland) Welfare Order 1926	S.R. & O. 1926/535 (S.24)	The whole Order
The Herring Curing Welfare Order 1927	S.R. & O. 1927/813, amended by S.I. 1960/1690 and 917	The whole Order

(1) Title	(2) Reference	(3) Extent of revocation
The Sacks (Cleaning and Repairing) Welfare Order 1927	S.R. & O. 1927/860	The whole Order
The Horizontal Milling Machines Regulations 1928	S.R. & O. 1928/548	The whole Regulations
The Cotton Cloth Factories Regulations 1929	S.I. 1929/300	Regulations 5 to 10, 11 and 12
The Oil Cake Welfare Order 1929	S.R. & O. 1929/534	Articles 3 to 6
The Cement Works Welfare Order 1930	S.R. & O. 1930/94	The whole Order
The Tanning Welfare Order 1930	S.R. & O. 1930/312	The whole Order
The Kiers Regulations 1938	S.R. & O. 1938/106, amended by S.I. 1981/1152	Regulations 12 to 15
The Sanitary Accommodation Regulations 1938	S.R. & O. 1938/611, amended by S.I. 1974/426	The whole Regulations
The Clay Works (Welfare) Special Regulations 1948	S.I. 1948/1547	Regulations 3, 4, 6, 8 and 9
The Jute (Safety, Health and Welfare) Regulations 1948	S.I. 1948/1696, amended by S.I. 1988/1657	Regulations 11, 13, 14 to 16 and 19 to 26

(1) *Title*	(2) *Reference*	(3) *Extent of revocation*
The Pottery (Health and Welfare) Special Regulations 1950	S.I. 1950/65, amended by S.I. 1963/879, 1973/36, 1980/1248, 1982/877, 1988/1657, 1989/2311 and 1990/305	Regulation 15
The Iron and Steel Foundries Regulations 1953	S.I. 1953/1464, amended by S.I. 1974/1681 and 1981/1332	The whole Regulations
The Washing Facilities (Running Water) Exemption Regulations 1960	S.I. 1960/1029	The whole Regulations
The Washing Facilities (Miscellaneous Industries) Regulations 1960	S.I. 1960/1214	The whole Regulations
The Factories (Cleanliness of Walls and Ceilings) Order 1960	S.I. 1960/1794, amended by S.I. 1974/427	The whole Order
The Non-ferrous Metals (Melting and Founding) Regulations 1962	S.I. 1962/1667, amended by S.I. 1974/1681, 1981/1332 and 1988/165	Regulations 5, 6 to 10, 14 to 17 and 20
The Offices, Shops and Railway Premises Act 1963 (Exemption No. 1) Order 1964	S.I. 1964/964	The whole Order
The Washing Facilities Regulations 1964	S.I. 1964/965	The whole Regulations

(1) Title	(2) Reference	(3) Extent of revocation
The Sanitary Conveniences Regulations 1964	S.I. 1964/966, amended by S.I. 1982/827	The whole Regulations
The Offices, Shops and Railway Premises Act 1963 (Exemption No. 7) Order 1968	S.I. 1968/1947, amended by S.I. 1982/827	The whole Order
The Abrasive Wheels Regulations 1970	S.I. 1970/535	Regulation 17
The Sanitary Accommodation (Amendment) Regulations 1974	S.I. 1974/426	The whole Regulations
The Factories (Cleanliness of Walls and Ceilings) (Amendment) Regulations 1974	S.I. 1974/427	The whole Regulations
The Woodworking Machines Regulations 1974	S.I. 1974/903, amended by S.I. 1978/1126	Regulations 10 to 12
The Offices, Shops and Railway Premises Act 1963 etc. (Metrication) Regulations 1982	S.I. 1982/827	The whole Regulations

APPENDIX 9

THE HEALTH AND SAFETY (DISPLAY SCREEN EQUIPMENT) REGULATIONS 1992

(S.I. 1992 No. 2792)

Made	*5th November 1992*
Laid before Parliament	*16th November 1992*
Coming into force	*1st January 1993*

The Secretary of State, in exercise of the powers conferred on her by sections 15(1), (2), (5)(b) and (9) and 82(3)(a) of, and paragraphs 1(1)(a) and (c) and (2), 7, 8(1), 9 and 14 of Schedule 3 to, the Health and Safety at Work etc. Act 1974[1] and of all other powers enabling her in that behalf and for the purpose of giving effect without modifications to proposals submitted to her by the Health and Safety Commission under section 11(2)(d) of the said Act after the carrying out by the said Commission of consultations in accordance with section 50(3) of that Act, hereby makes the following Regulations: **A9–01**

---

[1] 1974 c.37; sections 15(1) and 50(3) were amended by the Employment Protection Act 1975 (c.71), Schedule 15, paragraphs 6 and 16(3) respectively.

Citation, commencement, interpretation and application

A9–02 **1.** — (1) These Regulations may be cited as the Health and Safety (Display Screen Equipment) Regulations 1992 and shall come into force on 1st January 1993.

(2) In these Regulations —

(a) "display screen equipment" means any alphanumeric or graphic display screen, regardless of the display process involved;

(b) "operator" means a self-employed person who habitually uses display screen equipment as a significant part of his normal work;

(c) "use" means use for or in connection with work;

(d) "user" means an employee who habitually uses display screen equipment as a significant part of his normal work; and

(e) "workstation" means an assembly comprising —

(i) display screen equipment (whether provided with software determining the interface between the equipment and its operator or user, a keyboard or any other input device),

(ii) any optional accessories to the display screen equipment,

(iii) any disk drive, telephone, modem, printer, document holder, work chair, work desk, work surface or other item peripheral to the display screen equipment, and

(iv) the immediate work environment around the display screen equipment.

(3) Any reference in these Regulations to —

(a)   a numbered regulation is a reference to the regulation in these Regulations so numbered; or

(b)   a numbered paragraph is a reference to the paragraph so numbered in the regulation which the reference appears.

(4) Nothing in these Regulations shall apply to or in relation to —

(a)   drivers' cabs or control cabs for vehicles or machinery;

(b)   display screen equipment on board a means of transport;

(c)   display screen equipment mainly intended for public operation;

(d)   portable systems not in prolonged use;

(e)   calculators, cash registers or any equipment having a small data or measurement display required for direct use of the equipment; or

(f)   window typewriters.

Analysis of workstations

2. — (1) Every employer shall perform a suitable and sufficient   **A9–03** analysis of those workstations which —

(a)   (regardless of who has provided them) are used for the purposes of his under-taking by users; or

(b)   have been provided by him and are used for the purposes of his undertaking by operators,

for the purpose of assessing the health and safety risks to which those persons are exposed in consequence of that use.

(2) Any assessment made by an employer in pursuance of paragraph (1) shall be reviewed by him if —

(a)   there is reason to suspect that it is no longer valid; or

(b)   there has been a significant change in the matters to which it relates;

and where as a result of any such review changes to an assessment are required, the employer concerned shall make them.

(3) The employer shall reduce the risks identified in consequence of an assessment to the lowest extent reasonably practicable.

(4) The reference in paragraph (3) to "an assessment" is a reference to an assessment made by the employer concerned in pursuance of paragraph (1) and changed by him where necessary in pursuance of paragraph (2).

Requirements for workstations

A9–04   **3.** — (1) Every employer shall ensure that any workstation first put into service on or after 1st January 1993 which —

(a)   (regardless of who has provided it) may be used for the purposes of his under-taking by users; or

(b)   has been provided by him and may be used for the purposes of his undertaking by operators,

meets the requirements laid down in the Schedule to these Regulations to the extent specified in paragraph 1 thereof.

(2) Every employer shall ensure that any workstation first put into service on or before 31st December 1992 which —

(a)   (regardless of who has provided it) may be used for the purposes of his undertaking by users; or

(b)   was provided by him and may be used for the purposes of his undertaking by operators,

meets the requirements laid down in the Schedule to these Regulations to the extent specified in paragraph 1 thereof not later than 31st December 1996.

Daily work routine of users

4. Every employer shall so plan the activities of users at work in his undertaking that their daily work on display screen equipment is periodically interrupted by such breaks or changes of activity as reduce their workload at that equipment. **A9–05**

Eyes and eyesight

5. — (1) Where a person — **A9–06**

    (a)   is already a user on the date of coming into force of these Regulations; or

    (b)   is an employee who does not habitually use display screen equipment as a significant part of his normal work but is to become a user in the undertaking in which he is already employed,

his employer shall ensure that he is provided at his request with an appropriate eye and eyesight test, any such test to be carried out by a competent person.

(2) Any eye and eyesight test provided in accordance with paragraph (1) shall —

    (a)   in any case to which sub-paragraph (a) of that paragraph applies, be carried out as soon as practicable after being requested by the user concerned; and

    (b)   in any case to which sub-paragraph (b) of that paragraph applies, be carried out before the employee concerned becomes a user.

(3) At regular intervals after an employee has been provided with an eye and eyesight test in accordance with paragraphs (1) and (2), his employer shall, subject to paragraph (6), ensure that he is provided with a further eye and eyesight test of an appropriate nature, any such test to be carried out by a competent person.

(4) Where a user experiences visual difficulties which may reasonably be considered to be caused by work on display screen equipment, his employer shall ensure that he is provided at his request with an appropriate eye and eyesight test, any such test to be carried out by a competent person as soon as practicable after being requested as aforesaid.

(5) Every employer shall ensure that each user employed by him is provided with special corrective appliances appropriate for the work being done by the user concerned where —

(a)   normal corrective appliances cannot be used; and

(b)   the result of any eye and eyesight test which the user has been given in accordance with this regulation shows such provision to be necessary.

(6) Nothing in paragraph (3) shall require an employer to provide any employee with an eye and eyesight test against that employee's will.

Provision of training

A9–07   6. — (1) Where a person —

(a)   is already a user on the date of coming into force of these Regulations; or

(b)   is an employee who does not habitually use display screen equipment as a significant part of his normal work but is to become a user in the undertaking in which he is already employed,

his employer shall ensure that he is provided with adequate health and safety training in the use of any workstation upon which he may be required to work.

(2) Every employer shall ensure that each user at work in his undertaking is provided with adequate health and safety training

whenever the organisation of any workstation in that undertaking upon which he may be required to work is substantially modified.

Provision of information

7. — (1) Every employer shall ensure that operators and users at work in his undertaking are provided with adequate information about —   **A9–08**

    (a)   all aspects of health and safety relating to their work-stations; and

    (b)   such measures taken by him in compliance with his duties under regulations 2 and 3 as relate to them and their work.

(2) Every employer shall ensure that users at work in his under-taking are provided with adequate information about such measures taken by him in compliance with his duties under regulations 4 and 6(2) as relate to them and their work.

(3) Every employer shall ensure that users employed by him are provided with adequate information about such measures taken by him in compliance with his duties under regulations 5 and 6(1) as relate to them and their work.

Exemption certificates

8. — (1) The Secretary of State for Defence may, in the interests of national security, exempt any of the home forces, any visiting force or any headquarters from any of the requirements imposed by these Regulations.   **A9–10**

(2) Any exemption such as is specified in paragraph (1) may be granted subject to conditions and to a limit of time and may be revoked by the Secretary of State for Defence by a further certificate in writing at any time.

(3) In this regulation —

(a) "the home forces" has the same meaning as in section 12(1) of the Visiting Forces Act 1952[2];

(b) "headquarters" has the same meaning as in article 3(2) of the Visiting Forces and International Headquarters (Application of Law) Order 1965[3]; and

(c) "visiting force" has the same meaning as it does for the purposes of any provision of Part I of the Visiting Forces Act 1952.

Extension outside Great Britain

A9–11 **9.** These Regulations shall, subject to regulation 1(4), apply to and in relation to the premises and activities outside Great Britain to which sections 1 to 59 and 80 to 82 of the Health and Safety at Work etc. Act 1974 apply by virtue of the Health and Safety at Work etc. Act 1974 (Application Outside Great Britain) Order 1989[4] as they apply within Great Britain.

THE SCHEDULE   Regulation 3
(WHICH SETS OUT THE MINIMUM
REQUIREMENTS FOR WORKSTATIONS
WHICH ARE CONTAINED IN THE ANNEX TO
COUNCIL DIRECTIVE 90/270/EEC ON THE
MINIMUM SAFETY AND HEALTH
REQUIREMENTS FOR WORK WITH DISPLAY
SCREEN EQUIPMENT[5]

A9–12 **1.** Extent to which employers must ensure that workstations meet the requirements laid down in this schedules

---

[2]1952 c.7.
[3]S.I. 1965/1536, to which there are amendments not relevant to these Regulations.
[4]S.I. 1989/840.
[5]OJ No. L156, 21.6.90, p.14.

An employer shall ensure that a workstation meets the requirements laid down in this Schedule to the extent that —

(a) those requirements relate to a component which is present in the workstation concerned;

(b) those requirements have effect with a view to securing the health, safety and welfare of persons at work; and

(c) the inherent characteristics of a given task make compliance with those requirements appropriate as respects the workstation concerned.

2. Equipment

A9–13

(a) *General comment*
The use as such of the equipment must not be a source of risk for operators or users.

(b) *Display screen*
The characters on the screen shall be well-defined and clearly formed, of adequate size and with adequate spacing between the characters and lines.
The image on the screen should be stable, with no flickering or other forms of instability.
The brightness and the contrast between the characters and the background shall be easily adjustable by the operator or user, and also be easily adjustable to ambient conditions.
The screen must swivel and tilt easily and freely to suit the needs of the operator or user. It shall be possible to use a separate base for the screen or an adjustable table.
The screen shall be free of reflective glare and reflections liable to cause discomfort to the operator or user.

(c) *Keyboard*
The keyboard shall be tiltable and separate from the screen so as to allow the operator or user to find a comfortable working position avoiding fatigue in the arms or hands.
The space in front of the keyboard shall be sufficient to provide support for the hands and arms of the operator or user.

The keyboard shall have a matt surface to avoid reflective glare.

The arrangement of the keyboard and the characteristics of the keys shall be such as to facilitate the use of the keyboard.

The symbols on the keys shall be adequately contrasted and legible from the design working position.

(d) *Work desk or work surface*

The work desk or work surface shall have a sufficiently large, low-reflectance surface and allow a flexible arrangement of the screen, keyboard, documents and related equipment.

The document holder shall be stable and adjustable and shall be positioned so as to minimise the need for uncomfortable head and eye movements.

There shall be adequate space for operators or users to find a comfortable position.

(e) *Work chair*

The work chair shall be stable and allow the operator or user easy freedom of movement and a comfortable position.

The seat shall be adjustable in height.

The seat back shall be adjustable in both height and tilt.

A footrest shall be made available to any operator or user who wishes one.

A9–14   3. Environment

(a) *Space requirements*

The workstation shall be dimensioned and designed so as to provide sufficient space for the operator or user to change position and vary movements.

(b) *Lighting*

Any room lighting or task lighting provided shall ensure satisfactory lighting conditions and an appropriate contrast between the screen and the background environment, taking into account the type of work and the vision requirements of the operator or user.

Possible disturbing glare and reflections on the screen or other equipment shall be prevented by co-ordinating workplace and workstation layout with the positioning and technical characteristics of the artificial light sources.

(c) *Reflections and glare*
Workstations shall be so designed that sources of light, such as windows and other openings, transparent or translucid walls, and brightly coloured fixtures or walls cause no direct glare and no distracting reflections on the screen.
Windows shall be fitted with a suitable system of adjustable covering to attenuate the daylight that falls on the workstation.

(d) *Noise*
Noise emitted by equipment belonging to any workstation shall be taken into account when a workstation is being equipped, with a view in particular to ensuring that attention is not distracted and speech is not disturbed.

(e) *Heat*
Equipment belonging to any workstation shall not produce excess heat which could cause discomfort to operators or users.

(f) *Radiation*
All radiation with the exception of the visible part of the electromagnetic spectrum shall be reduced to negligible levels from the point of view of the protection of operators' or users' health and safety.

(g) *Humidity*
An adequate level of humidity shall be established and maintained.

4. Interface between computer and operator/user   A9–15

In designing, selecting, commissioning and modifying software, and in designing tasks using display screen equipment, the employer shall take into account the following principles:

(a) software must be suitable for the task;

(b) software must be easy to use and, where appropriate, adaptable to the level of knowledge or experience of the operator or user; no quantitative or qualitative checking facility may be used without the knowledge of the operators or users;

(c)   systems must provide feedback to operators or users on the performance of those systems;

(d)   systems must display information in a format and at a pace which are adapted to operators or users;

(e)   the principles of software ergonomics must be applied, in particular to human data processing.

APPENDIX 10

THE MANUAL HANDLING OPERATIONS REGULATIONS 1992

(S.I. 1992 No. 2793)

Made	*5th November 1992*
Laid before Parliament	*16th November 1992*
Coming into force	*1st January 1993*

The Secretary of State, in exercise of the powers conferred on her by   **A10–01**
sections 15(1) (2), (3)(a),(5)(a) and (9) and 80(1), (2)(a) and (4) of;
and paragraphs (1)(a) and (c) and 8 of Schedule 3 to, the Health and
Safety at Work etc.Act 1974[1] ("the 1917 Act") and of all other
powers enabling her in that behalf and —

    (a)   for the purpose of giving effect without modifications to
          proposals submitted to her by the Health and Safety Com-
          mission under section 11(2)(d) of the 1974 Act after the
          carrying out by the said Commission of consultations in
          accordance with section 50(3) of that Act; and

    (b)   it appearing to her that the repeal of section 18(1) of the
          Children and Young Persons Act 1933[2] and section

---

[1] 1974c. 37; sections 15(1), 50(3) and 80(4) were amended by the Employment
Protection Act 1975 (c.71), Schedule 15, paragraphs 6, 16(3) and 19 respectively.
[2] 1933 c. 12.

28(1)(f) of the Children and Young Persons (Scotland) Act 1937[3] except insofar as those provisions apply to such employment as is permitted under section 1(2) of the Employment of Women, Young Persons, and Children Act 1920[4] is expedient in consequence of the Regulations referred to below after the carrying out by her of consultations in accordance with section 80(4) of the 1974 Act,

hereby makes the following Regulations:

Citation and commencement

1. These Regulations may be cited as the Manual Handling Operations Regulations 1992 and shall come into force on 1st January 1993.

Interpretation

A10–02 **2.** — (1) In these Regulations, unless the context otherwise requires —

"injury" does not include injury caused by any toxic or corrosive substance which —

(a)   has leaked or spilled from a load;

(b)   is present on the surface of a load but has not leaked or spilled from it; or

(c)   is a constituent part of a load;

and "injured" shall be construed accordingly;
"load" includes any person and any animal;

---

[3]1937 c. 37.
[4]1920 c. 65.

"manual handling operations" means any transporting or supporting of a load (including the lifting, putting down, pushing, pulling, carrying or moving thereof) by hand or by bodily force

(2) Any duty imposed by these Regulations on an employer in respect of his employees shall also be imposed on a self-employed person in respect of himself.

Disapplication of Regulations

3. These Regulations shall not apply to or in relation to the master or crew of a sea-going ship or to the employer of such persons in respect of the normal ship-board activities of a ship's crew under the direction of the master.

Duties of employers

4. — (1) Each employer shall —   A10–03

    (a)   so far as is reasonably practicable, avoid the need for his employees to undertake any manual handling operations at work which involve a risk of their being injured; or

    (b)   where it is not reasonably practicable to avoid the need for his employees to undertake any manual handling operations at work which involve a risk of their being injured —

        (i)   make a suitable and sufficient assessment of all such manual handling operations to be undertaken by them, having regard to the factors which are specified in column 1 of Schedule 1 to these Regulations and considering the questions which are specified in the corresponding entry in column 2 of that Schedule,

        (ii)   take appropriate steps to reduce the risk of injury to those employees arising out of their undertaking any such manual handling operations to the lowest level reasonably practicable, and

(iii) take appropriate steps to provide any of those employees who are undertaking any such manual handling operations with general indications and, where it is reasonably practicable to do so, precise information on —

(aa) the weight of each load, and

(bb) the heaviest side of any load whose centre of gravity is not positioned centrally.

(2) Any assessment such as is referred to in paragraph (1)(b)(i) of this regulation shall be reviewed by the employer who made it it —

(a)   there is reason to suspect that it is no longer valid; or

(b)   there has been a significant change in the manual handling operations to which it relates;

and where as a result of any such review changes to an assessment are required, the relevant employer shall make them.

Duty of employees

5. Each employee while at work shall make full and proper use of any system of work provided for his use by his employer in compliance with regulation 4(1)(b)(ii) of these Regulations.

Exemption certificates

A10–04 **6.** — (1) The Secretary of State for Defence may, in the interests of national security, by a certificate in writing exempt —

(a)   any of the home forces, any visiting force or any headquarters from any requirement imposed by regulation 4 of
these Regulations; or

(b)   any member of the home forces, any member of a visiting
force or any member of a headquarters from the requirement imposed by regulation 5 of these Regulations;

and any exemption such as is specified in sub-paragraph (a) or (b) of
this paragraph may be granted subject to conditions and to a limit of
time and may be revoked by the said Secretary of State by a further
certificate in writing at any time.

(2) In this regulation —

(a)   "the home forces" has the same meaning as in section
12(1) of the Visiting Forces Act 1952[5];

(b)   "headquarters" has the same meaning as in article 3(2) of
the Visiting Forces and International Headquarters
(Application of Law) Order 1965[6];

(c)   "member of a headquarters" has the same meaning as in
paragraph 1(1) of the Schedule to the International Headquarters and Defence Organisations Act 1964[7]; and

(d)   "visiting force" has the same meaning as it does for the
purposes of any provision of Part I of the Visiting Forces
Act 1952.

Extension outside Great Britain

7. These Regulations shall, subject to regulation 3 hereof, apply to   **A01–05**
and in relation to the premises and activities outside Great Britain to
which sections 1 to 59 and 80 to 82 of the Health and Safety at Work

---

[5]1952 c. 67.
[6]S.I. 1965/1536, to which there are amendments not relevant to these Regulations.
[7]1964 c. 5.

etc. Act 1974 apply by virtue of the Health and Safety at Work etc. Act 1974 (Application Outside Great Britain) Order 1989[8] as they apply within Great Britain.

Repeals and revocations

8. — (1) The enactments mentioned in column 1 of Part I of Schedule 2 to these Regulations are repealed to the extent specified in the corresponding entry in column 3 of that part.

(2) The Regulations mentioned in column 1 of Part I of Schedule 2 to these Regulations are repealed to the extent specified in the corresponding entry in column 3 of that part.

---

[8]S.I. 1989/840.

SCHEDULE 1 Regulation 4(1)(b)(i)
FACTORS TO WHICH THE EMPLOYER MUST HAVE REGARD AND QUESTIONS HE MUST CONSIDER WHEN MAKING AN ASSESSMENT OF MANUAL HANDLING OPERATIONS

A10–06

Column 1 *Factors*	Column 2 *Questions*

1. The tasks	**Do they involve:**
	—holding or manipulating loads at distance from trunk?
	—unsatisfactory bodily movement or posture, especially:
	    —twisting the trunk?
	    —stooping?
	    —reaching upwards?
	—excessive movement of loads, especially:
	    —excessive lifting or lowering distances?
	    —excessive carrying distances?
	—excessive pushing or pulling of loads?
	—risk of sudden movement of loads?
	—frequent or prolonged physical effort?
	—insufficient rest or recovery periods?
	—a rate of work imposed by a process?

2. The loads	**Are they:** —heavy? —bulky or unwieldy? —difficult to grasp? —unstable, or with contents likely to shift? —sharp, hot or otherwise potentially damaging?
3. The working environment	**Are there:** —space constraints preventing good posture? —uneven, slippery or unstable floors? —variations in level of floors or work surfaces? —extremes of temperature or humidity? —conditions causing ventilation problems or gusts of wind? —poor lighting conditions?

Column 1 *Factors*	Column 2 *Questions*
4. Individual capability	**Does the job:** —require unusual strength, height, etc? —create a hazard to those who might reasonably be considered to be pregnant or to have a health problem? —require special information or training for its safe performance?
5. Other factors	**Is movement or posture hindered by personal protective equipment or by clothing?**

SCHEDULE 2 Regulation 8
REPEALS AND REVOCATIONS

PART I

REPEALS

A10–07

Column 1 *Short title of enactment*	Column 2 *Reference*	Column 3 *Extent of repeal*
The Children and Young Persons Act 1933.	1933 c.12.	Section 18(1)(f) except insofar as that paragraph applies to such employment as is permitted under section 1(2) of the Employment of Women, Young Persons, and Children Act 1920 (1920 c.65).
The Children and Young Persons (Scotland) Act 1937	1937 c.37.	Section 28(1)(f) except insofar as that paragraph applies to such employment as is permitted under section 1(2) of the Employment of Women, Young Persons, and Children Act 1920.
The Mines and Quarries Act 1954.	1954 c.70.	Section 93; in section 115 the word "ninety-three".
The Agriculture (Safety, Health and Welfare Provisions) Act 1956.	1956 c.49.	Section 2.
The Factories Act 1961.	1961 c.34.	Section 72.

Column 1 *Short title of enactment*	Column 2 *Reference*	Column 3 *Extent of repeal*
The Offices, Shops and Railway Premises Act 1963	1963 c.41.	Section 23 except insofar as the prohibition contained in that section applies to any person specified in section 90(4) of the same Act. In section 83(1) the number "23".

PART II

REVOCATIONS

A10–08

Column 1 *Title of instrument*	Column 2 *Reference*	Column 3 *Extent of revocation*
The Agriculture (Lifting of Heavy Weights) Regulations 1959.	S.I. 1959/2120.	The whole Regulations.
The Construction (General Provisions) Regulations 1961.	S.I. 1961/1580.	In regulation 3(1)(a) the phrase "and 55"; regulation 55.

APPENDIX 11

THE PROVISION AND USE OF WORK EQUIPMENT REGULATIONS 1992

(S.I. 1992 No. 2932)

Made	*17th November 1992*
Laid before Parliament	*30th November 1992*
Coming into force	
The whole Regulations except regulations 11 to 24 and 27 and Schedule 2 to the extent specified in regulation 1(3)	*1st January 1993*
Regulations 11 to 24 and 27 and Schedule 2 to the extent specified in regulation 1(3)	*1st January 1997*

ARRANGEMENT OF REGULATIONS

225

The Secretary of State, in the exercise of the powers conferred on her by sections 15(1), (2), (3)(a), (5)(b) and (9), and 82(3)(a) of, and paragraphs 1(1), (2) and (3), 13(1) and 14 of Schedule 3 to, the Health and Safety at Work etc. Act 1974[1] ("the 1974 Act") and of all other powers enabling her in that behalf and for the purpose of giving effect without modifications to proposals submitted to her by the Health and Safety Commission under section 11(2)(d) of the 1974 Act, after the carrying out by the said Commission of consultations in accordance with section 50(3) of that Act, hereby makes the following Regulations:

Citation and commencement

1. — (1) These Regulations may be cited as the Provision and Use of Work Equipment Regulations 1992. **A11–02**

(2) Subject to paragraph (3), these Regulations shall come into force on 1st January 1993.

(3) Regulations 11 to 24 and 27 and Schedule 2 in so far as they apply to work equipment first provided for use in the premises or undertaking before 1st January 1993 shall come into force on 1st January 1997.

Interpretation

2. — (1) In these Regulations, unless the context otherwise requires — **A11–03**

---

[1] 1974 c.37; sections 15 and 50 were amended by the Employment Protection Act 1975 (c.71), Schedule 15, paragraphs 6 and 16 respectively. The general purposes of Part I of the 1974 Act were extended by section 1(1) of the Offshore Safety Act 1992. (c.15).

"use" in relation to work equipment means any activity involving work equipment and includes starting, stopping, programming, setting, transporting, repairing, modifying, maintaining, servicing and cleaning, and related expressions shall be construed accordingly;

"work equipment" means any machinery, appliance, apparatus or tool and any assembly of components which, in order to achieve a common end, are arranged and controlled so that they function as a whole.

(2) Any reference in these Regulations to —

(a) a numbered regulation or Schedule is a reference to the regulation or Schedule in these Regulations so numbered; and

(b) a numbered paragraph is a reference to the paragraph so numbered in the regulation in which the reference appears.

Disapplication of these Regulations

A11–04 **3.** These Regulations shall not apply to or in relation to the master or crew of a seagoing ship or to the employer of such persons, in respect of the normal ship-board activities of a ship's crew under the direction of the master.

Application of requirements under these Regulations

A11–05 **4.** — (1) The requirements imposed by these Regulations on an employer shall apply in respect of work equipment provided for use or used by any of his employees who is at work or who is on an offshore installation within the meaning assigned to that term by section 1(4) of the Offshore Safety Act 1992[2].

---

[2] 1992 c.15.

(2) The requirements imposed by these Regulations on an employer shall also apply —

(a) to a self-employed person, in respect of work equipment he uses at work;

(b) to any person who has control, to any extent, of non-domestic premises made available to persons as a place of work, in respect of work equipment used in such premises by such persons and to the extent of his control; and

(c) to any person to whom the provisions of the Factories Act 1961[3] apply by virtue of section 175(5) of that Act as if he were the occupier of a factory, in respect of work equipment used in the premises deemed to be a factory by that section.

(3) Any reference in paragraph (2)(b) to a person having control of any premises or matter is a reference to the person having control of the premises or matter in connection with the carrying on by him of a trade, business or other undertaking (whether for profit or not).

Suitability of work equipment

5. — (1) Every employer shall ensure that work equipment is so **A11–06** constructed or adapted as to be suitable for the purpose for which it is used or provided.

(2) In selecting work equipment, every employer shall have regard to the working conditions and to the risks to the health and safety of persons which exist in the premises or undertaking in which that work equipment is to be used and any additional risk posed by the use of that work equipment.

(3) Every employer shall ensure that work equipment is used only for operations for which, and under conditions for which, it is suitable.

(4) In this regulation "suitable" means suitable in any respect which it is reasonably foreseeable will affect the health or safety of any person.

---

[3] 1961 c.34.

Maintenance

A11–07 **6.** — (1) Every employer shall ensure that work equipment is maintained in an efficient state, in efficient working order and in good repair.

(2) Every employer shall ensure that where any machinery has a maintenance log, the log is kept up to date.

Specific risks

A11–08 **7.** — (1) Where the use of work equipment is likely to involve a specific risk to health or safety, every employer shall ensure that —

(a) the use of that work equipment is restricted to those persons given the task of using it; and

(b) repairs, modifications, maintenance or servicing of that work equipment is restricted to those persons who have been specifically designated to perform operations of that description (whether or not also authorised to perform other operations).

(2) The employer shall ensure that the persons designated for the purposes of subparagraph (b) of paragraph (1) have received adequate training related to any operations in respect of which they have been so designated.

Information and instructions

A11–09 **8.** — (1) Every employer shall ensure that all persons who use work equipment have available to them adequate health and safety information and, where appropriate, written instructions pertaining to the use of the work equipment.

(2) Every employer shall ensure that any of his employees who supervises or manages the use of work equipment has available to

him adequate health and safety information and, where appropriate, written instructions pertaining to the use of the work equipment.

(3) Without prejudice to the generality of paragraphs (1) or (2), the information and instructions required by either of those paragraphs shall include information and, where appropriate, written instructions on —

(a)   the conditions in which and the methods by which the work equipment may be used;

(b)   foreseeable abnormal situations and the action to be taken if such a situation were to occur; and

(c)   any conclusions to be drawn from experience in using the work equipment.

(4) Information and instructions required by this regulation shall be readily comprehensible to those concerned.

Training

9. — (1) Every employer shall ensure that all persons who use work equipment have received adequate training for purposes of health and safety, including training in the methods which may be adopted when using the work equipment, any risks which such use may entail and precautions to be taken.   **A11–10**

(2) Every employer shall ensure that any of his employees who supervises or manages the use of work equipment has received adequate training for purposes of health and safety, including training in the methods which may be adopted when using the work equipment, any risks which such use may entail and precautions to be taken.

Conformity with Community requirements

10. — (1) Every employer shall ensure that any item of work equipment provided for use in the premises or undertaking of the   **A11–11**

employer complies with any enactment (whether in an Act or instrument) which implements in Great Britain any of the relevant Community directives listed in Schedule 1 which is applicable to that item of work equipment.

(2) Where it is shown that an item of work equipment complies with an enactment (whether in an Act or instrument) to which it is subject by virtue of paragraph (1), the requirements of regulations 11 to 24 shall apply in respect of that item of work equipment only to the extent that the relevant Community directive implemented by that enactment is not applicable to that item of work equipment.

(3) This regulation applies to items of work equipment provided for use in the premises or undertaking of the employer for the first time after 31st December 1992.

Dangerous parts of machinery

A11–12 **11.** — (1) Every employer shall ensure that measures are taken in accordance with paragraph (2) which are effective —

(a)   to prevent access to any dangerous part of machinery or to any rotating stockbar; or

(b)   to stop the movement of any dangerous part of machinery or rotating stockbar before any part of a person enters a danger zone.

(2) The measures required by paragraph (1) shall consist of —

(a)   the provision of fixed guards enclosing every dangerous part or rotating stockbar where and to the extent that it is practicable to do so, but where or to the extent that it is not, then

(b)   the provision of other guards or protection devices where and to the extent that it is practicable to do so, but where or to the extent that it is not, then

(c)   the provision of jigs, holders, push-sticks or similar protection appliances used in conjunction with the machinery where and to the extent that it is practicable to do so, but where or to the extent that it is not, then

(d)   the provision of information, instruction, training and supervision.

(3) All guards and protection devices provided under sub-paragraphs (a) or (b) of paragraph (2) shall —

(a)   be suitable for the purpose for which they are provided;

(b)   be of good construction, sound material and adequate strength;

(c)   be maintained in an efficient state, in efficient working order and in good repair;

(d)   not give rise to any increased risk to health or safety;

(e)   not be easily bypassed or disabled;

(f)   be situated at sufficient distance from the danger zone;

(g)   not unduly restrict the view of the operating cycle of the machinery, where such a view is necessary;

(h)   be so constructed or adapted that they allow operations necessary to fit or replace parts and for maintenance work, restricting access so that it is allowed only to the area where the work is to be carried out and, if possible, without having to dismantle the guard or protection device.

(4) All protection appliances provided under sub-paragraph (c) of paragraph (2) shall comply with sub-paragraphs (a) to (d) and (g) of paragraph (3).

(5) In this regulation —

"danger zone" means any zone in or around machinery in which a person is exposed to a risk to health or safety from contact with a dangerous part of machinery or a rotating stock-bar;

"stock-bar" means any part of a stock-bar which projects beyond the head-stock of a lathe.

Protection against specified hazards

A11–13 **12.** — (1) Every employer shall take measures to ensure that the exposure of a person using work equipment to any risk to his health or safety from any hazard specified in paragraph (3) is either prevented, or, where that is not reasonably practicable, adequately controlled.

(2) The measures required by paragraph (1) shall —

(a) be measures other than the provision of personal protective equipment or of information, instruction, training and supervision, so far as is reasonably practicable; and

(b) include, where appropriate, measures to minimise the effects of the hazard as well as to reduce the likelihood of the hazard occurring.

(3) The hazards referred to in paragraph (1) are —

(a) any article or substance falling or being ejected from work equipment;

(b) rupture or disintegration of parts of work equipment;

(c) work equipment catching fire or overheating;

(d) the unintended or premature discharge of any article or of any gas, dust, liquid, vapour or other substance which, in each case, is produced, used or stored in the work equipment;

(e) the unintended or premature explosion of the work equipment or any article or substance produced, used or stored in it.

(4) For the purposes of this regulation "adequate" means adequate having regard only to the nature of the hazard and the nature and degree of exposure to the risk, and "adequately" shall be construed accordingly.

(5) This regulation shall not apply where any of the following Regulations apply in respect of any risk to a person's health or safety for which such Regulations require measures to be taken to prevent or control such risk, namely —

(a)   the Control of Lead at Work Regulations 1980[4];

(b)   the Ionising Radiations Regulations 1985[5];

(c)   the Control of Asbestos at Work Regulations 1987[6];

(d)   the Control of Substances Hazardous to Health Regulations 1988[7];

(e)   the Noise at Work Regulations 1989[8];

(f)   the Construction (Head Protection) Regulations 1989[9].

High or very low temperature

13. Every employer shall ensure that work equipment, parts of work equipment and any article or substance produced, used or stored in work equipment which, in each case, is at a high or very low temperature shall have protection where appropriate so as to prevent injury to any person by burn, scald or sear.   **A11–14**

Controls for starting or making a significant change in operating conditions

14. — (1) Every employer shall ensure that, where appropriate, work equipment is provided with one or more controls for the purposes of —   **A11–15**

---

[4]S.I. 1980/1248.
[5]S.I. 1985/1333.
[6]S.I. 1987/2115; amended by S.I. 1988/712.
[7]S.I. 1988/1657; amended by S.I. 1990/2026 and S.I. 1991/2431..
[8]S.I. 1989/1790.
[9]S.I. 1989/2209.

(a) starting the work equipment (including re-starting after a stoppage for any reason); or

(b) controlling any change in the speed, pressure or other operating conditions of the work equipment where such conditions after the change result in risk to health and safety which is greater than or of a different nature from such risks before the change.

(2) Subject to paragraph (3), every employer shall ensure that where a control is required by paragraph (1), it shall not be possible to perform any operation mentioned in sub-paragraph (a) or (b) of that paragraph except by a deliberate action on such control.

(3) Paragraph (1) shall not apply to re-starting or changing operating conditions as a result of the normal operating cycle of an automatic device.

Stop controls

A11–16 **15.** — (1) Every employer shall ensure that, where appropriate, work equipment is provide with one or more readily accessible controls the operation of which will bring the work equipment to a safe condition in a safe manner.

(2) Any control required by paragraph (1) shall bring the work equipment to a complete stop where necessary for reasons of health and safety.

(3) Any control required by paragraph (1) shall, if necessary for reasons of health and safety, switch off all sources of energy after stopping the functioning of the work equipment.

(4) Any control required by paragraph (1) shall operate in priority to any control which starts or changes the operating conditions of the work equipment.

Emergency stop controls

A11–17 **16.** — (1) Every employer shall ensure that, where appropriate, work equipment is provided with one or more readily accessible emergency stop controls unless it is not necessary by reason of the nature

236

of the hazards and the time taken for the work equipment to come to a complete stop as a result of the action of any control provided by virtue of regulation 15(1).

(2) Any control required by paragraph (1) shall operate in priority to any control required by regulation 15(1).

Controls

17. — (1) Every employer shall ensure that all controls for work equipment shall be clearly visible and identifiable, including by appropriate marking where neccessary.   **A11–18**

(2) Except where necessary, the employer shall ensure that no control for work equipment is in a position where any person operating the control is exposed to a risk to his health or safety.

(3) Every employer shall ensure where appropriate —

(a)   that, so far as is reasonably practicable, the operator of any control is able to ensure from the position of that control that no person is in a place where he would be exposed to any risk to his health or safety as a result of the operation of that control, but where or to the extent that it is not reasonably practicable;

(b)   that, so far as is reasonably practicable, systems of work are effective to ensure that, when work equipment is about to start, no person is in a place where he would be exposed to a risk to his health or safety as a result of the work equipment starting, but where neither of these is reasonably practicable;

(c)   that an audible, visible or other suitable warning is given by virtue of regulation 24 whenever work equipment is about to start.

(4) Every employer shall take appropriate measures to ensure that any person who is in a place where he would be exposed to a risk to

his health or safety as a result of the starting or stopping of work equipment has sufficient time and suitable means to avoid that risk.

Control systems

A11–19 **18.** — (1) Every employer shall ensure, so far as is reasonably practicable, that all control systems of work equipment are safe.

(2) Without prejudice to the generality of paragraph (1), a control system shall not be safe unless —

(a)   its operation does not create any increased risk to health or safety;

(b)   it ensures, so far as is reasonably practicable, that any fault in or damage to any part of the control system or the loss of supply of any source of energy used by the work equipment cannot result in additional or increased risk to health or safety;

(c)   it does not impede the operation of any control required by regulation 15 or 16.

Isolation from sources of energy

A11–20 **19.** — (1) Every employer shall ensure that where appropriate work equipment is provided with suitable means to isolate it from all its sources of energy.

(2) Without prejudice to the generality of paragraph (1), the means mentioned in that paragraph shall not be suitable unless they are clearly identifiable and readily accessible.

(3) Every employer shall take appropriate measures to ensure that re-connection of any energy source to work equipment does not expose any person using the work equipment to any risk to his health or safety.

Stability

20. Every employer shall ensure that work equipment or any part of   **A11–21**
work equipment is stabilised by clamping or otherwise where necessary for purposes of health or safety.

Lighting

21. Every employer shall ensure that suitable and sufficient lighting,   **A11–22**
which takes account of the operations to be carried out, is provided at
any place where a person uses work equipment.

Maintenance operations

22. Every employer shall take appropriate measures to ensure that   **A11–23**
work equipment is so constructed or adapted that, so far as is
reasonably practicable, maintenance operations which involve a risk
to health or safety can be carried out while the work equipment is
shut down or, in other cases —

(a)   maintenance operations can be carried out without expos-
ing the person carrying them out to a risk to his health or
safety; or

(b)   appropriate measures can be taken for the protection of
any person carrying out maintenance operations which
involve a risk to his health or safety.

Markings

23. Every employer shall ensure that work equipment is marked in a   **A11–24**
clearly visible manner with any marking appropriate for reasons of
health and safety.

Warnings

A11–25 **24.** — (1) Every employer shall ensure that work equipment incorporates any warnings or warning devices which are appropriate for reasons of health and safety.

(2) Without prejudice to the generality of paragraph (1), warnings given by warning devices on work equipment shall not be appropriate unless they are unambiguous, easily perceived and easily understood.

Exemption certificates

A11–26 **25.** — (1) The Secretary of State for Defence may, in the interests of national security, by a certificate in writing exempt any of the home forces, any visiting force or any headquarters from any of the requirements of these Regulations and any such exemption may be granted subject to conditions and to a limit of time and may be revoked by the said Secretary of State by a further certificate in writing at any time.

(2) In this regulation —

(a) "the home forces" has the same meaning as in section 12(1) of the Visiting Forces Act 1952[10];

(b) "headquarters" has the same meaning as in article 3(2) of the Visiting Forces and International Headquarters (Application of Law) Order 1965[11];

(c) "visiting force" has the same meaning as it does for the purposes of any provision of Part I of the Visiting Forces Act 1952.

---

[10]1952 c.67.
[11]S.I. 1965/1536, to which there are amendments not relevant to these regulations.

Extension outside Great Britain

26. These Regulations shall, subject to regulation 3, apply to and in relation to the premises and activities outside Great Britain to which sections 1 to 59 and 80 to 82 of the 1974 Act apply by virtue of the Health and Safety at Work etc. Act 1974 (Application outside Great Britain) Order 1989[12] as they apply within Great Britain.   **A11–27**

Repeals, saving and revocations

27. — (1) Subject to paragraph (2), the enactments mentioned in Part I of Schedule 2 are repealed to the extent specified in column 3 of that Part.   **A11–28**

(2) Nothing in this regulation shall affect the operation of any provision of the Offices, Shops and Railway Premises Act 1963[13] as that provision has effect by virtue of section 90(4) of that Act.

(3) The instruments mentioned in Part II of Schedule 2 are revoked to the extent specified in column 3 of that Part.

SCHEDULE 1   Regulation 10
RELEVANT COMMUNITY DIRECTIVES

1. Council Directive 73/23/EEC on the harmonization of the laws of Member States relating to electrical equipment designed for use within certain voltage limits (OJ No. L77, 26.3.1973, p.29).   **A11–29**

2. Council Directive 79/113/EEC on the approximation of the laws of the Member States relating to the determination of the noise emission of construction plant and equipment (OJ No. L33, 8.2.1979, p.15).

3. Council Directive 81/1051/EEC amending Directive 79/113/EEC on the approximation of the laws of the Member States relating to the determination of the noise emission of construction plant and equipment (OJ No. L376, 30.12.1981, p.49).

---

[12]S.I. 1989/840.
[13]1963 c.41.

4. Council Directive 84/532/EEC on the approximation of the laws of the Member States relating to common provisions for construction plant and equipment (OJ No. L300, 19.11.1984, p.111).

5. Council Directive 84/533/EEC on the approximation of the laws of the Member States relating to the permissible sound power level of compressors (OJ No. L300, 19.11.1984, p.123).

6. Council Directive 84/534/EEC on the approximation of the laws of the Member States relating to the permissible sound power level of tower cranes (OJ No. L300, 19.11.1984, p.130).

7. Council Directive 84/535/EEC on the approximation of the laws of the Member States relating to the permissible sound power level of welding generators (OJ No. L300, 19.11.1984, p.142).

A11–30 **8.** Council Directive 84/536/EEC on the approximation of the laws of the Member States relating to the permissible sound power level of power generators (OJ No. L300, 19.11.1984, p.149).

9. Council Directive 84/537/EEC on the approximation of the laws of the Member States relating to the permissible sound power level of powered hand-held concrete-breakers and picks (OJ No. L300, 19.11.1984, p.156).

10. Council Directive 84/538/EEC on the approximation of the laws of the Member States relating to the permissible sound power level of lawn mowers (OJ No. L300, 19.11.1984, p.171).

11. Commission Directive 85/405/EEC adapting to technical progress Council Directive 79/113/EEC on the approximation of the laws of the Member States relating to the determination of the noise emission of construction plant and equipment (OJ No. L233, 30.8.1985, p.9).

12. Commission Directive 85/406/EEC adapting to technical progress Council Directive 84/533/EEC on the approximation of the laws of the Member States relating to the permissible sound power level of compressors (OJ No. L233, 30.8.1985, p.11).

13. Commission Directive 85/407/EEC adapting to technical progress Council Directive 84/535/EEC on the approximation of the laws of the Member States relating to the permissible sound power level of welding generators (OJ No. L233, 30.8.1985, p.16).

14. Commission Directive 85/408/EEC adapting to technical progress Council Directive 84/536/EEC on the approximation of the laws of the Member States relating to the permissible sound power level of power generators (OJ No. L233, 30.8.1985, p.18).

A11–31 **15.** Commission Directive 85/409/EEC adapting to technical progress Council Directive 84/537/EEC on the approximation of the laws of the Member States relating to the permissible sound power level of powered hand-held concrete-breakers and picks (OJ No. L233, 30.8.1985, p.20).

16. Commission Directive 87/252/EEC adapting to technical progress Council Directive 84/538/EEC on the approximation of the laws of the Member States relating to the permissible sound power level of lawn mowers (OJ No. L117, 5.5.1987, p.22 with corrigenda at OJ No. L158, 18.6.1987, p.31).

17. Council Directive 87/405/EEC amending Council Directive 84/534/EEC on the approximation of the laws of the Member States relating to the permissible sound power level of tower cranes (OJ No. L220, 8.8.1987, p.60).

18. Council Directive 88/180/EEC amending Council Directive 84/538/EEC on the approximation of the laws of the Member States relating to the permissible sound power level of lawn-mowers (OJ No. L81, 26.3.1988, p.69).

19. Council Directive 88/181/EEC amending Council Directive 84/538/EEC on the approximation of the laws of the Member States relating to the permissible sound power level of lawn-mowers (OJ No. L81, 26.3.1988, p.71).

20. Council Directive 84/539/EEC on the approximation of the laws of the Member States relating to electro-medical equipment used in human or veterinary medicine (OJ No. L300, 19.11.1984, p.179).

21. Council Directive 86/295/EEC on the approximation of the laws of the Member States relating to roll-over protective structures (ROPS) for certain construction plant (OJ No. L186, 8.7.1986, p.1).

22. Council Directive 86/296/EEC on the approximation of the laws **A11–32** of the Member States relating to falling-object protective structures (FOPS) for certain construction plant (OJ No. L186, 8.7.1986, p.10).

23. Council Directive 86/662/EEC on the limitation of noise emitted by hydraulic excavators, rope-operated excavators, dozers, loaders and excavator-loaders (OJ No. L384, 31.12.1986, p.1).

24. Council Directive 86/663/EEC on the approximation of the laws of the Member States relating to self-propelled industrial trucks (OJ No. L384, 31.12.1986, p.12).

25. Council Directive 87/404/EEC on the harmonization of the laws of the Member States relating to simple pressure vessels (OJ No. L220, 8.8.1987, p.48).

26. Council Directive 89/106/EEC on the approximation of laws, regulations and administrative provisions of the Member States relating to construction products OJ No. L40, dated 11.2.1989 p.12).

27. Commission Directive 89/240/EEC adapting to technical progress Council Directive 86/663/EEC on the approximation of the laws of the Member States relating to self-propelled industrial trucks (OJ No. L100, 12.4.1989, p.1).

28. Council Directive 89/336/EEC on the approximation of the laws of the Member States relating to electromagnetic compatibility (OJ No. L139, 23.5.1989, p.19).

A11–33 **29.** Council Directive 89/392/EEC on the approximation of the laws of the Member States relating to machinery (OJ No. L183, 29.6.1989, p.9).

30. Commission Directive 89/514/EEC adapting to technical progress Council Directive 86/662/EEC on the limitation of noise emitted by hydraulic excavators, rope-operated excavators, dozers, loaders and excavator-loaders (OJ No. L253, 30.8.1989, p.35).

31. Council Directive 89/686/EEC on the approximation of the laws of the Member States relating to personal protective equipment (OJ No. L399, 30.12.1989, p.18).

32. Council Directive 90/385/EEC on the approximation of the laws of the Member States relating to active implantable medical devices (OJ No. L189, 20.7.1990, p.17).

33. Council Directive 90/396/EEC on the approximation of the laws of the Member States relating to appliances burning gaseous fuels (OJ No. L196, 26.7.1990, p.15).

34. Council Directive 91/368/EEC amending Directive 89/392/EEC on the approximation of the laws of the Member States relating to machinery (OJ No. L198, 22.7.1991, p.16).

35. Council Directive 92/31/EEC amending Directive 89/336/EEC on the approximation of the laws of the Member States relating to electromagnetic compatibility (OJ No. L126, 12.5.92, p.11).

SCHEDULE 2   Regulation 27

PART I

REPEALS

A11–34

(1) *Chapter*	(2) *Short title*	(3) *Extent of repeal*
1954 c.70.	The Mines and Quarries Act 1954.	Sections 81(1) and 82.
1961 c.34.	The Factories Act 1961.	Sections 12 to 16, 17 and 19.
1963 c.41.	The Offices, Shops and Railway Premises Act 1963.	Section 17.

PART II

REVOCATIONS

A11–35

(1) *Title*	(2) *Reference*	(3) *Extent of revocation*
Regulations dated 17th October 1905 (The Spinning by Self-Acting Mules Regulations 1905).	S.R. & O. 1905/1103, amended by the Employment Act 1989 (c.38), section 29(5), Schedule 8.	The whole Regulations.

(1) Title	(2) Reference	(3) Extent of revocation
The Aerated Water Regulations 1921.	S.R. & O. 1921/1932, amended by S.I. 1981/686.	Regulations 1, 2 and 8.
The Horizontal Milling Machines Regulations 1928.	S.R. & O. 1928/548, amended by S.R. & O. 1934/207.	The exemptions and regulations 2 to 7.
The Operations at Unfenced Machinery Regulations 1938.	S.R. & O. 1938/641, amended by S.R. & O. 1946/156 and S.I. 1976/955.	The whole Regulations.
The Jute (Safety, Health and Welfare) Regulations 1948.	S.I. 1948/1696, to which there are amendments not relevant to these Regulations.	Regulations 15, 27 and 28 and the First Schedule.
The Iron and Steel Foundries Regulations 1953.	S.I. 1953/1464, amended by S.I. 1974/1681 and S.I. 1981/1332.	Regulation 5.
The Agriculture (Power Take-Off) Regulations 1957.	S.I. 1957/1386, amended by S.I. 1976/1247, S.I. 1981/1414 and S.I. 1991/1913.	The whole Regulations.

(1) *Title*	(2) *Reference*	(3) *Extent of revocation*
The Agriculture (Circular Saws) Regulations 1959.	S.I. 1959/427, amended by S.I. 1981/1414.	(i) In regulation 1, in sub-paragraph (b), from the beginning to "and" where it first occurs; and sub-paragraph (c); (ii) regulations 3 and 4; (iii) in regulation 5(1), the words from "unless" to "or"; and (iv) Schedule 1.
The Agriculture (Stationary Machinery) Regulations 1959.	S.I. 1959/1216, amended by S.I. 1976/1247 and S.I. 1981/1414.	The whole Regulations.
The Agriculture (Threshers and Balers) Regulations 1960.	S.I. 1960/1199, amended by S.I. 1976/1247 and S.I. 1981/1414.	In the Schedule, paragraphs 2, 3, 6, 7, 8, 9, 10, 11, 12, 16 and 17.
The Shipbuilding and Ship-Repairing Regulations 1960.	S.I. 1960/1932, to which there are amendments not relevant to these Regulations.	Regulation 67.
The Construction (General Provisions) Regulations 1961.	S.I. 1961/1580, to which there are amendments not relevant to these Regulations.	Regulations 42, 43 and 57.

(1) Title	(2) Reference	(3) Extent of revocation
The Agriculture (Field Machinery) Regulations 1962.	S.I. 1962/1472, amended by S.I. 1976/1247 and S.I. 1981/1414.	In the Schedule, paragraphs 2 to 6 and 15 to 19.
The Abrasive Wheels Regulations 1970.	S.I. 1970/535.	In regulation 3, paragraphs (2), (3) and (4); and regulations 4, 6 to 8, 10 to 16, 18 and 19.
The Woodworking Machines Regulations 1974.	S.I. 1974/903, amended by S.I. 1978/1126.	In regulation 1, paragraphs (2) and (3); in regulation 2, the definitions of "cutters", "machine table", "narrow band sawing machine", "sawmill" and "squared stock"; in regulation 3, paragraph (2); regulations 5 to 9, 14 to 19, 21 to 38, and 40 to 43.
The Offshore Installations (Operational Safety, Health and Welfare) Regulations 1976.	S.I. 1976/1019, which has effect as an existing statutory provision under the 1974 Act by virtue of section 1(1) of the Offshore Safety Act 1992 (c.15).	Regulations 10 and 12.
The Agriculture (Power Take-off) (Amendment) Regulations 1991.	S.I. 1991/1913.	The whole Regulations.

APPENDIX 12

THE PERSONAL PROTECTIVE EQUIPMENT AT WORK REGULATIONS 1992

(S.I. 1992 No. 2966)

Made	*25th November 1992*
Laid before Parliament	*2nd December 1992*
Coming into force	*1st January 1993*

ARRANGEMENT OF REGULATIONS

249

8. Accommodation for personal protective equipment

9. Information, instruction and training

10. Use of personal protective equipment

11. Reporting loss or defect

12. Exemption certificates

13. Extension outside Great Britain

14. Modifications, repeal and revocations

Schedule 1: Relevant Community directive

Schedule 2: Modifications

Part I The Factories Act 1961

Part II The Coal and Other Mines (Fire and Rescue) Order 1956

Part III The Shipbuilding and Ship-Repairing Regulations 1960

Part IV The Coal Mines (Respirable Dust) Regulations 1975

Part V The Control of Lead at Work Regulations 1980

Part VI The Ionising Radiations Regulations 1985

Part VII The Control of Asbestos at Work Regulations 1987

Part VIII The Control of Substances Hazardous to Health Regulations 1988

Part IX The Noise at Work Regulations 1989

Part X The Construction (Head Protection) Regulations 1989

Schedule 3 Revocations

The Secretary of State, in exercise of the powers conferred upon her by sections 15(1). (2), (3)(a) and (b), (5)(b) and (9) of, and paragraphs 11 and 14 of Schedule 3 to the Health and Safety at Work etc.

Act 1974[1], and of all other powers enabling her in that behalf and for the purpose of giving effect without modifications to proposals submitted to her by the Health and Safety Commission under section 11(2)(d) of the said Act after the carrying out by the said Commission of consultations in accordance with section 50(3) of that Act, hereby makes the following Regulations:

Citation and Commencement

1. These Regulations may be cited as the Personal Protective Equipment at Work Regulations 1992 and shall come into force on 1st January 1993.

A12–02

Interpretation

2. — (1) In these Regulations, unless the context otherwise requires. "personal protective equipment" means all equipment (including clothing affording protection against the weather) which is intended to be worn or held by a person at work and which protects him against one or more risks to his health or safety, and any addition or accessory designed to meet that objective.

A12–03

(2) Any reference in these Regulations to —

(a) a numbered regulation or Schedule is a reference to the regulation or Schedule in these Regulations so numbered; and

(b) a numbered paragraph is a reference to the paragraph so numbered in the regulation in which the reference appears.

---

[1] 1974 c.37; sections 15 and 50 were amended by the Employment Protection Act 1975 (c.71), Schedule 15, paragraphs 6 and 16 respectively.

Disapplication of these Regulations

A12–04 3. — (1) These Regulations shall not apply to or in relation to the master or crew of a sea-going ship or to the employer of such persons in respect of the normal ship-board activities of a ship's crew under the direction of the master.

(2) Regulations 4 to 12 shall not apply in respect of personal protective equipment which is —

    (a)   ordinary working clothes and uniforms which do not specifically protect the health and safety of the wearer;

    (b)   an offensive weapon within the meaning of section 1(4) of the Prevention of Crime Act 1953[2] used as self-defence or as deterrent equipment;

    (c)   portable devices for detecting and signalling risks and nuisances;

    (d)   personal protective equipment used for protection while travelling on a road within the meaning (in England and Wales) of section 192(1) of the Road Traffic Act 1988[3], and (in Scotland) of section 151 of the Roads (Scotland) Act 1984[4];

    (e)   equipment used during the playing of competitive sports.

(3) Regulations 4 and 6 to 12 shall not apply where any of the following Regulations apply and in respect of any risk to a person's health or safety for which any of them require the provision or use of personal protective equipment, namely —

    (a)   the Control of Lead at Work Regulations 1980;[5]

    (b)   the Ionising Radiations Regulations 1985;[6]

---

[2] 1953 c.14.
[3] 1988 c.52.
[4] 1984 c.54.
[5] S.I. 1980/1248.
[6] S.I. 1985/1333.

(c)   the Control of Asbestos at Work Regulations 1987;[7]

(d)   the Control of Substances Hazardous to Health Regulations 1988;[8]

(e)   the Noise at Work Regulations 1989;[9]

(f)   the Construction (Head Protection) Regulations 1989[10].

Provision of personal protective equipment

4. — (1) Every employer shall ensure that suitable personal protective equipment is provided to his employees who may be exposed to a risk to their health or safety while at work except where and to the extent that such risk has been adequately controlled by other means which are equally or more effective.

(2) Every self-employed person shall ensure that he is provided with suitable personal protective equipment where he may be exposed to a risk to his health or safety while at work except where and to the extent that such risk has been adequately controlled by other means which are equally or more effective.

(3) Without prejudice to the generality of paragraphs (1) and (2), personal protective equipment shall not be suitable unless —

A12–05

(a)   it is appropriate for the risk or risks involved and the conditions at the place where exposure to the risk may occur;

(b)   it takes account of ergonomic requirements and the state of health of the person or persons who may wear it;

(c)   it is capable of fitting the wearer correctly, if necessary, after adjustments within the range for which it is designed;

---

[7]S.I. 1987/2115; amended by S.I. 1988/712.
[8]S.I. 1988/1657; amended by S.I. 1990/2026 and S.I. 1992/2382.
[9]S.I. 1989/1790.
[10]S.I. 1989/2209.

(d) so far as is practicable, it is effective to prevent or adequately control the risk or risks involved without increasing overall risk;

(e) it complies with any enactment (whether in an Act or instrument) which implements in Great Britain any provision on design or manufacture with respect to health or safety in any relevant Community directive listed in Schedule 1 which is applicable to that item of personal protective equipment.

Compatibility of personal protective equipment

A12–06   **5.** — (1) Every employer shall ensure that where the presence of more than one risk to health or safety makes it necessary for his employee to wear or use simultaneously more than one item of personal protective equipment, such equipment is compatible and continues to be effective against the risk or risks in question.

(2) Every self-employed person shall ensure that where the presence of more than one risk to health or safety makes it necessary for him to wear or use simultaneously more than one item of personal protective equipment, such equipment is compatible and continues to be effective against the risk or risks in question.

Assessment of personal protective equipment

A12–07   **6.** — (1) Before choosing any personal protective equipment which by virtue of regulation 4 he is required to ensure is provided, an employer or self-employed person shall ensure that an assessment is made to determine whether the personal protective equipment he intends will be provided is suitable.

(2) The assessment required by paragraph (1) shall include —

(a) an assessment of any risk or risks to health or safety which have not been avoided by other means;

(b) the definition of the characteristics which personal protective equipment must have in order to be effective against the risks referred to in sub-paragraph (a) of this paragraph, taking into account any risks which the equipment itself may create;

(c) comparison of the characteristics of the personal protective equipment available with the characteristics referred to in sub-paragraph (b) of this paragraph.

(3) Every employer or self-employed person who is required by paragraph (1) to ensure that any assessment is made shall ensure that any such assessment is reviewed if —

(a) there is reason to suspect that it is no longer valid; or

(b) there has been a significant change in the matters to which it relates,

and where as a result of any such review changes in the assessment are required, the relevant employer or self-employed person shall ensure that they are made.

Maintenance and replacement of personal protective equipment

7. — (1) Every employer shall ensure that any personal protective **A12–08** equipment provided to his employees is maintained (including replaced or cleaned as appropriate) in an efficient state, in efficient working order and in good repair.

(2) Every self-employed person shall ensure that any personal protective equipment provided to him is maintained (including replaced or cleaned as appropriate) in an efficient state, in efficient working order and in good repair.

Accommodation for personal protective equipment

8. — (1) Where an employer or self-employed person is required, by **A12–09** virtue of regulation 4, to ensure personal protective equipment is

255

provided, he shall also ensure that appropriate accommodation is provided for that personal protective equipment when it is not being used.

Information, instruction and training

A12–10 **9.** — (1) Where an employer is required to ensure that personal protective equipment is provided to an employee, the employer shall also ensure that the employee is provided with such information, instruction and training as is adequate and appropriate to enable the employee to know —

    (a)   the risk or risks which the personal protective equipment will avoid or limit;

    (b)   the purpose for which and the manner in which personal protective equipment is to be used; and

    (c)   any action to be taken by the employee to ensure that the personal protective equipment remains in an efficient state, in efficient working order and in good repair as required by regulation 7(1).

(2) Without prejudice to the generality of paragraph (1), the information and instruction provided by virtue of that paragraph shall not be adequate and appropriate unless it is comprehensible to the persons to whom it is provided.

Use of personal protective equipment

A12–11 **10.** — (1) Every employer shall take all reasonable steps to ensure that any personal protective equipment provided to his employees by virtue of regulation 4(1) is properly used.

(2) Every employee shall use any personal protective equipment provided to him by virtue of these Regulations in accordance both

with any training in the use of the personal protective equipment concerned which has been received by him and the instructions respecting that use which have been provided to him by virtue of regulation 9.

(3) Every self-employed person shall make full and proper use of any personal protective equipment provided to him by virtue of regulation 4(2).

(4) Every employee and self-employed person who has been provided with personal protective equipment by virtue of regulation 4 shall take all reasonable steps to ensure that it is returned to the accommodation provided for it after use.

Reporting loss or defect

11. Every employee who has been provided with personal protective   **A12–12**
equipment by virtue of regulation 4(1) shall forthwith report to his employer any loss of or obvious defect in that personal protective equipment.

Exemption certificates

12. — (1) The Secretary of State for Defence may, in the interests of   **A12–13**
national security, by a certificate in writing exempt —

(a)   any of the home forces, any visiting force or any head-quarters from those requirements of these Regulations which impose obligations on employers; or

(b)   any member of the home forces, any member of a visiting force or any member of a headquarters from the require-ments imposed by regulation 10 or 11;

and any exemption such as is specified in sub-paragraph (a) or (b) of this paragraph may be granted subject to conditions and to a limit of time and may be revoked by the said Secretary of State by a further certificate in writing at any time.

(2) In this regulation —

(a) "the home forces" has the same meaning as in section 12(1) of the Visiting Forces Act 1952[11];

(b) "headquarters" has the same meaning as in article 3(2) of the Visiting Forces and International Headquarters (Application of Law) Order 1965[12];

(c) "member of a headquarters" has the same meaning as in paragraph 1(1) of the Schedule to the International Headquarters and Defence Organisations Act 1964[13]; and

(d) "visiting force" has the same meaning as it does for the purposes of any provision of Part I of the Visiting Forces Act 1952.

Extension outside great britain

A12–14 **13.** These Regulations shall apply to and in relation to the premises and activities outside Great Britain to which sections 1 to 59 and 80 to 82 of the Health and Safety at Work etc. Act 1974 apply by virtue of the Health and Safety at Work etc. Act 1974 (Application Outside Great Britain) Order 1989[14] as they apply within Great Britain.

Modifications, repeal and revocations

A12–15 **14.** — (1) The Act and Regulations specified in Schedule 2 shall be modified to the extent specified in the corresponding Part of that Schedule.

---

[11]1952 c.67.
[12]S.I. 1965/1536, to which there are amendments not relevant to these Regulations.
[13]1964 c.5.
[14]S.I. 1989/840.

(2) Section 65 of the Factories Act 1961 is repealed.

(3) The instruments specified in column 1 of Schedule 3 are revoked to the extent specified in column 3 of that Schedule.

SCHEDULE 1

Regulation 4(3)(e)

RELEVANT COMMUNITY DIRECTIVE

Council Directive of 21 December 1989 on the approximation of the laws of the Member States relating to personal protective equipment (89/686/EEC)[15]. **A12–16**

SCHEDULE 2

Regulation 14(1)

MODIFICATIONS

PART I

THE FACTORIES ACT 1961[16]

1. In section 30(6), for "breathing apparatus of a type approved by the chief inspector", substitute "suitable breathing apparatus". **A12–17**

---

[15]O.J. L399, 30.12.89, p. 18.

[16]1961 c.34; in section 30(6), by virtue of S.I. 1974/1941, references to the chief inspector are to be construed as references to an inspector appointed by the Health and Safety Executive under section 19 of the Health and Safety at Work etc. Act 1974 who is authorised to act for the purposes of the provision in question.

PART II

THE COAL AND OTHER MINES (FIRE AND RESCUE) ORDER 1956[17]

A12–18 **2.** In Schedule 1, in regulation 23(a), for "breathing apparatus of a type approved by the Minister", substitute "suitable breathing apparatus".

3. In Schedule 1, in regulation 23(b), for "smoke helmets or other apparatus serving the same purpose, being helmets or apparatus of a type approved by the Minister,", substitute "suitable smoke helmets or other suitable apparatus serving the same purpose".

4. In Schedule 1, in regulation 24(a), for "smoke helmet or other apparatus serving the same purpose, being a helmet or other apparatus of a type approved by the Minister,", substitute "suitable smoke helmet or other suitable apparatus serving the same purpose".

PART III

TTHE SHIPBUILDING AND SHIP-REPAIRING REGULATIONS 1960

A12–19 **5.** In each of regulations 50, 51(1) and 60(1), for "breathing apparatus of a type approved for the purpose of this Regulation", substitute "suitable breathing apparatus".

PART IV

THE COAL MINES (RESPIRABLE DUST) REGULATIONS 1975[18]

A12–20 **6.** In regulation 10(a), for "dust respirators of a type approved by the Executive for the purpose of this Regulation", substitute "suitable dust respirators".

---

[17]S.I. 1956/1768; to which there are amendments not relevant to these Regulations.
[18]S.I. 1975/1433; to which there are amendments not relevant to these Regulations.

PART V

THE CONTROL OF LEAD AT WORK REGULATIONS 1980

7. In regulation 7 —

   (a)   after "respiratory protective equipment", insert "which complies with regulation 8A or, where the requirements of that regulation do not apply, which is"; and

   (b)   after "as will", insert ", in either case,".

8. In regulation 8, for "adequate protective clothing", substitute "protective clothing which complies with regulation 8A or, where no requirement is imposed by virtue of that regulation, is adequate".

9. After regulation 8, insert the following new regulation —

"Compliance with relevant Community directives

8A. Any respiratory protective equipment or protective clothing shall comply with any enactment (whether in an Act or instrument) which implements any provision on design or manufacture with respect to health or safety in any relevant Community directive listed in Schedule 1 to the Personal Protective Equipment at Work Regulations 1992 which is applicable to that item of respiratory protective equipment or protective clothing.

Assessment of respiratory protective equipment or protective clothing

8B. — (1) Before choosing respiratory protective equipment or protective clothing, an employer shall make an assessment to determine whether it will satisfy regulation 7 or 8, as appropriate.

(2) The assessment required by paragraph (1) shall involve —

   (a)   definition of the characteristics necessary to comply with regulation 7 or, as the case may be, 8, and

   (b)   comparison of the characteristics of respiratory protective equipment or protective clothing available with the characteristics referred to in sub-paragraph (a) of this paragraph.

(3) The assessment required by paragraph (1) shall be revised if —

(a) there is reason to suspect that it is no longer valid; or

(b) there has been a significant change in the work to which it relates.
and, where, as a result of the review, changes in the assessment are required, the employer shall make them.".

10. In regulation 9, for sub-paragraph (b), substitute the following sub-paragraph —
"(b) where he is required under regulations 7 or 8 to provide respiratory protective equipment or protective clothing, adequate changing facilities and adequate facilities for the storage of —

(i) the respiratory protective equipment or protective clothing, and

(ii) personal clothing not worn during working hours.".

11. At the end of regulation 13, add the following new paragraph —
"(3) Every employee shall take all reasonable steps to ensure that any respiratory protective equipment provided to him pursuant to regulation 7 and protective clothing provided to him pursuant to regulation 8 is returned to the accommodation provided for it after use."

12. In regulation 18(2), omit the full stop and add "and that any provision imposed by the European Communities in respect of the encouragement of improvements in the safety and health of workers at work will be satisfied.".

PART VI

THE IONISING RADIATIONS REGULATIONS 1985

A12–22 **13.** In regulation 23(1), after "that respiratory protective equipment", insert "complies with paragraph (1A) or, where no requirement is imposed by that paragraph,".
14. After regulation 23(1), insert the following paragraphs —
"(1A) For the purposes of paragraph (1), personal protective equipment complies with this paragraph if it complies with any enactment (whether in an Act or instrument) which implements

in Great Britain any provision on design or manufacture with respect to health or safety in any relevant Community directive listed in Schedule 1 to the Personal Protective Equipment at Work Regulations 1992 which is applicable to that item of personal protective equipment.

(1B) Before choosing personal protective equipment, an employer shall make an assessment to determine whether it will satisfy regulation 6(3).

(1C) The assessment required by paragraph (1B) shall involve —

(a) definition of the characteristics necessary to comply with regulation 6(3), and

(b) comparison of the characteristics of available personal protective equipment with the characteristics referred to in sub-paragraph (a) of this paragraph.

(1D) The assessment required by paragraph (1B) shall be reviewed if —

(a) there is reason to suspect that it is no longer valid; or

(b) there has been a significant change in the work to which it relates,
and where, as a result of the review, changes in the assessment are required, the employer shall make them.".

15. Add at the end of regulation 23 the following additional paragraphs —

"(2A) Every employer shall ensure that appropriate accommodation is provided for personal protective equipment when it is not being worn.

(2B) Every employee shall take all reasonable steps to ensure that personal protective equipment provided to him is returned to the accommodation provided for it after use.".

PART VII

THE CONTROL OF ASBESTOS AT WORK REGULATIONS 1987

16. In regulation 8(3), after "shall" the first time that word appears, insert "comply with paragraph (3A) or, where no requirement is imposed by that paragraph, shall".

A12–23

17. Insert the following new paragraph after regulation 8(3) —

"(3A) Any respiratory protective equipment provided in pursuance of paragraph (2) or protective clothing provided in pursuance of regulation 11(1) shall comply with this paragraph if it complies with any enactment (whether in an Act or instrument) which implements in Great Britain any provision on design or manufacture with respect to health or safety in any relevant Community directive listed in Schedule 1 to the Personal Protective Equipment at Work Regulations 1992 which is applicable to that item of respiratory protective equipment or protective clothing.".

18. In regulation 20(2), omit the fullstop and add "and that any provision imposed by the European Communities in respect of the encouragement of improvements in the safety and health of workers at work will be satisfied.".

PART VIII

THE CONTROL OF SUBSTANCES HAZARDOUS TO HEALTH REGULATIONS 1988

A12–24 **19.** In regulation 7, after paragraph (3), insert the following new paragraph —

"(3A) Any personal protective equipment provided by an employer in pursuance of this regulation shall comply with any enactment (whether in an Act or instrument) which implements in Great Britain any provision on design or manufacture with respect to health or safety in any relevant Community directive listed in Schedule 1 to the Personal Protective Equipment at Work Regulations 1992 which is applicable to that item of personal protective equipment.".

20. In regulation 7, in paragraph (6)(b), insert at the beginning "complies with paragraph (3A) or, where no requirement is imposed by virtue of that paragraph,".

21. In regulation 8(2), after "these regulations", insert "and shall take all reasonable steps to ensure it is returned after use to any accommodation provided for it".

PART IX

THE NOISE AT WORK REGULATIONS 1989

22. Add the following new paragraph at the end of regulation 8 —   **A12–25**
"(3) Any personal ear protectors provided by virtue of this regulation shall comply with any enactment (whether in an Act or instrument) which implements in Great Britain any provision on design or manufacture with respect to health or safety in any relevant Community directive listed in Schedule 1 to the Personal Protective Equipment at Work Regulations 1992 which is applicable to those ear protectors.".

PART X

THE CONSTRUCTION (HEAD PROTECTION) REGULATIONS 1989

23. Add the following paragraphs at the end of regulation 3 —   **A12–26**
"(3) Any head protection provided by virtue of this regulation shall comply with any enactment (whether in an Act or instrument) which implements any provision on design or manufacture with respect to health or safety in any relevant Community directive listed in Schedule 1 to the Personal Protective Equipment at Work Regulations 1992 which is applicable to that head protection.

(4) Before choosing head protection, an employer of self-employed person shall make an assessment to determine whether it is suitable.

(5) The assessment required by paragraph (4) of this regulation shall involve —

(a)   the definition of the characteristics which head protection must have in order to be suitable;

(b)   comparison of the characteristics of the protection available with the characteristics referred to in sub-paragraph (a) of this paragraph.

(6) The assessment required by paragraph (4) shall be reviewed if —

(a)   there is reason to suspect that it is no longer valid; or

(b)   there has been a significant change in the work to which it relates,
and where as a result of the review changes in the assessment are required, the relevant employer or self-employed person shall make them.

(7) Every employer and every self-employed person shall ensure that appropriate accommodation is available for head protection provided by virtue of these Regulations when it is not being used.''.

24. For regulation 6(4), substitute the following paragraph —
''(4) Every employee or self-employed person who is required to wear suitable head protection by or under these Regulations shall —

(a)   make full and proper use of it; and

(b)   take all reasonable steps to return it to the accommodation provided for it after use.''.

25. In regulation 9(2), omit the full stop and add ''and that any provision imposed by the European Communities in respect of the encouragement of improvements in the safety and health of workers at work will be satisfied.''.

SCHEDULE 3
REVOCATIONS

Regulation 14(3)

A12–27

(1) *Title*	(2) *Reference*	(3) *Extent of Revocation*
Regulations dated 26th February 1906 in respect of the processes of spinning and weaving of flax and tow and the processes incidental thereto (the Flax and Tow-Spinning and Weaving Regulations 1906).	S.R. & O. 1906/177, amended by S.I. 1988/1657.	In regulation 9, the words "unless waterproof skirts, and bibs of suitable material, are provided by the occupier and worn by the workers". Regulation 13.
Order dated 5th October 1917 (the Tin or Terne Plates Manufacture Welfare Order 1917).	S.R. & O. 1917/1035.	Paragraph 1.
Order dated 15th August 1919 (the Fruit Preserving Welfare Order 1919).	S.R. & O. 1919/1136, amended by S.I. 1988/1657.	Paragraph 1.
Order dated 23rd April 1920 (the Laundries Welfare Order 1920).	S.R. & O. 1920/654.	Paragraph 1.
Order dated 28th July 1920 (the Gut-Scrapping, Tripe Dressing, etc. Welfare Order 1920).	S.R. & O. 1920/1437.	Paragraph 1.
Order dated 3rd March 1921 (the Glass Bevelling Welfare Order 1921).	S.R. & O. 1921/288.	Paragraph 1.

(1) Title	(2) Reference	(3) Extent of Revocation
The Aerated Water Regulations 1921.	S.R. & O. 1921/1932; amended by S.I. 1981/686.	The whole Regulations.
The Sacks (Cleaning and Repairing) Welfare Order 1927.	S.R. & O. 1927/860.	Paragraph 1.
The Oil Cake Welfare Order 1929.	S.R. & O. 1929/534.	Paragraph 1.
The Cement Works Welfare Order 1930.	S.R. & O. 1930/94.	Paragraph 1.
The Tanning Welfare Order 1930.	S.R. & O. 1930/312.	Paragraph 1 and the Schedule.
The Magnesium (Grinding of Castings and Other Articles) Special Regulations 1946.	S.R. & O. 1946/2107.	Regulation 12.
The Clay Works (Welfare) Special Regulations 1948.	S.I. 1948/1547.	Regulation 5.
The Iron and Steel Foundries Regulations 1953.	S.I. 1953/1464; amended by S.I. 1974/1681 and S.I. 1981/1332.	Regulation 8.
The Shipbuilding and Ship-Repairing Regulations 1960.		Regulations 73 and 74.
The Non-Ferrous Metals (Melting and Founding) Regulations 1962.	S.I. 1962/1667; amended by S.I. 1974/1681.	Regulation 13.

(1) *Title*	(2) *Reference*	(3) *Extent of Revocation*
The Abstract of Special Regulations (Aerated Water) Order 1963.	S.I. 1963/2058.	The whole Order.
The Construction (Health and Welfare) Regulations 1966.	S.I. 1966/95; to which there are amendments not relevant to these regulations.	Regulation 15.
The Foundries (Protective Footwear and Gaiters) Regulations 1971.	S.I. 1971/476.	The whole Regulations.
The Protection of Eyes Regulations 1974.	S.I. 1974/1681; amended by S.I. 1975/303.	The whole Regulations.
The Aerated Water Regulations (Metrication) Regulations 1981.	S.I. 1981/686.	The whole Regulations.

INDEX

278